Company's Coming®

low-fat COOKING

Low-Fat Cooking

Second printing May 1998

Canadian Cataloguing in Publication Data
   Low-fat cooking
Issued also in French under title:
   La cuisine faible en gras
Includes index.
ISBN 1-896891-32-2
   1. Low-fat diet—Recipes. I. Title

RM237.7.P37 1998   641.5'638   C97-901251-1

Published simultaneously in Canada and the United States of America by The Recipe Factory Inc. in conjunction with Company's Coming Publishing Limited
2311 - 96 Street
Edmonton, Alberta, Canada
T6N 1G3
Tel: 403 • 450-6223
Fax: 403 • 450-1857

COOKBOOKS

Low-Fat Cooking was created thanks to the dedicated efforts of the people and organizations listed below.

COMPANY'S COMING PUBLISHING LIMITED

Chairperson
Jean Paré

President
Grant Lovig

V.P. Product Development
Kathy Knowles

Design Manager
Derrick Sorochan

Design
Jaclyn Draker
Nora Cserny

Copywriting/Project Assistant
Debbie Dixon

Typesetting
Marlene Crosbie

THE RECIPE FACTORY INC.

Research & Development Manager
Nora Prokop

Test Kitchen Supervisor
Lynda Elsenheimer

Editor
Stephanie Amodio

Food Stylist
Cora Lewyk

Assistant Editor
Michelle White

Photographer
Stephe Tate Photo

Prop Stylist
Gabriele McEleney

Color separations, printing, and binding by Friesens, Altona, Manitoba, Canada
Printed in Canada

Our special thanks to the following businesses for providing extensive props for photography.

Chintz & Company
Creations by Design
Dansk Gifts
Eaton's
Enchanted Kitchen
Kitchen Treasures
Le Gnome
Scona Clayworks
Stokes
The Basket House
The Bay
The Glasshouse
The Royal Doulton Store
Tile Town Ltd.
Wicker World
Winter Art Glass Studio Inc.

FRONT COVER

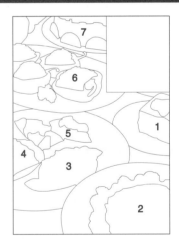

1. Tiramisu, page 63
2. Creamy Dijon Spinach Sauce, page 134
3. Tangy Roasted Veggies, page 154
4. Creamy Cucumber Cups, page 123
5. Tomato Sherry Chicken, page 95
6. Stuffed Peppers, page 96
7. Lemon Fluff Dessert, page 61

Table of contents

Company's Coming

cookbooks

COMPANY'S COMING SERIES

150 Delicious Squares
Casseroles
Muffins & More
Salads
Appetizers
Desserts
Soups & Sandwiches
Holiday Entertaining
Cookies
Vegetables
Main Courses
Pasta
Cakes
Barbecues

Dinners of the World
Lunches
Pies
Light Recipes
Microwave Cooking
Preserves
Light Casseroles
Chicken, Etc.
Kids Cooking
Fish & Seafood
Breads
Meatless Cooking
Cooking for Two
Breakfasts & Brunches

SELECT SERIES

Sauces & Marinades
Ground Beef
Beans & Rice

30-Minute Meals
Make-Ahead Salads
No-Bake Desserts

INDIVIDUAL TITLES

Company's Coming for Christmas
Beef Today!
The Family Table
Kids Only - Snacks
Low-Fat Cooking NEW!
Company's Coming for Kids - Lunches NEW July 1998

foreword

More and more people today are looking for ways to make their lifestyle healthier, and these recipes offer a great start! *Low-Fat Cooking* boasts over 150 fabulous recipes, each containing less than 10 grams of fat per serving. Although not intended to be a weight-loss book or diet plan, these recipes, along with proper exercise, can certainly be included as part of your healthy lifestyle.

In the next few pages you will find helpful calculations to show what percentage of calories from fat should be in your diet, and how to determine your maximum daily fat allowances. Learn the differences between saturated and unsaturated fats. Explore the many creative alternatives to high-fat products, and get the facts on product labels and how to read their nutrition information. Also included throughout the book are helpful tips and hints on easy low-fat cooking and preparation techniques.

Each recipe includes a nutrition analysis which identifies calories, total fat, protein and sodium content. To help you target high-risk fats, the total fat information has been broken down further into saturated fat and cholesterol. These analyses have been done using the ingredients listed in each recipe, with the exception of those identified as "optional" or "garnish". We have also used the first ingredient listed whenever a second alternative is offered (such as "butter or hard margarine"). If a range of servings is offered in a recipe, we analyzed the first serving amount, which is the larger serving size.

Inviting appetizers to decadent desserts—all of these recipes are unbelievably low in fat. Baked Spring Rolls or Saté With Peanut Sauce are great introductions to any meal. Whip up speedy Roasted Vegetable Focaccia or Beef Stroganoff for lunch or dinner, then complement it with luscious sweets such as Banana Butterscotch Cream Pie or Chocolate Mousse Parfait. Having guests over for tea or brunch? Think light and offer an assortment of low-fat muffins and coffee cakes.

Cover to cover, *Low-Fat Cooking* is brimming with creatively developed and tested recipes that taste great. What a delicious way to kick-start your healthy lifestyle!

each recipe

has been analyzed using the most updated version of the Canadian Nutrient File from Health and Welfare Canada, which is based upon the United States Department of Agriculture (USDA) Nutrient Data Base.

Margaret Ng, B.Sc. (Hon), M.A.
Registered Dietician

Facts About Fat

Calories are measurements of energy, and you need and get this energy on a daily basis from the nutrients in the foods you eat.

Fat, carbohydrates and protein are all energy nutrients, but fat offers a more concentrated source of energy (calories):

1 gram of fat = 9 calories
1 gram of protein = 4 calories
1 gram of carbohydrates = 4 calories

As you can see, fat contains over twice the amount of calories as carbohydrates or protein. How many calories your body requires is determined by a number of factors, including your size, weight and lifestyle. To find out how many calories are recommended for your daily intake, you should consult a dietician.

To maintain a healthy lifestyle it's recommended that no more than 30% of your daily energy intake come from fat, and no more than 10% of that should be saturated fat. This refers to **total daily food intake and not just individual foods.** So, it's okay to indulge in foods higher in fat, as long as you also eat foods lower in fat, for an average of 30% per day.

How can I find out what percentage of calories comes from fat in the foods I eat?

First, multiply the number of grams of fat in a food by 9 to get the number of fat calories.

Fat (grams) x 9 (calories/gram) = fat calories

Next, divide that number by the total number of calories in the food. Now multiply the result by 100:

(Fat calories ÷ total calories) X 100
= % calories from fat

For example: ¼ cup (60 mL) grated Cheddar cheese contains 113 calories and 9.3 grams of fat. Using this calculation, we can determine that:

9.3 grams x 9 calories/gram
= 83.7 fat calories
(83.7 fat calories ÷ 113 total calories)
X 100 = 74% calories from fat

I find that calculating the percentage is too cumbersome. How many grams of fat can I have each day?

Many people find it easier to calculate their daily allowance in grams instead of percentages. Here is a great guideline to follow:

Multiply your total recommended energy (calorie) intake by 30% (or 0.3), then divide by 9. As an example, suppose your energy intake is 1500 calories per day and your goal is 30% calories from fat:

1500 total calories x 0.30 from fat
= 500 fat calories
500 fat calories ÷ 9 calories/gram
= 56 grams of fat per day

With all the recipes in *Low-Fat Cooking* under 10 grams of fat per serving, a selection of 7 or 8 recipes throughout the day should keep you within the range of 40 to 70 grams per day.

Types of Fat

You are faced with different types of fat in your diet, and each has a different effect on the body.

Saturated fats are solid at room temperature. They are found in animal products (butter, cheese, milk, eggs, etc.), and in some tropical plants such as palm and coconut oils. Our bodies don't easily break down saturated fats, and it's this kind of fat that can be associated with certain forms of cancer, increased cholesterol levels and risk of heart disease.

Unsaturated fats (monounsaturated and polyunsaturated) are liquid at room temperature. They are considered to be less harmful than saturated fats, and may even help lower total cholesterol and triglyceride levels. Unfortunately, too much of this fat can also contribute to obesity, gallstones and certain cancers.

Hydrogenated fats start out as liquid but become solid when hydrogen bonds are added. This process converts a liquid oil into a more solid fat and creates trans-fatty acids, which have the same health effects as saturated fats. Hydrogenated oils are used to increase a product's shelf life because they resist breaking down when exposed to oxygen. Examples of these products are margarine, shortening and peanut butter.

Cholesterol is a wax-like substance that is produced naturally by your body and is found in foods of animal origin (meats, fish, poultry, eggs and dairy products). You need only a small amount of cholesterol to form hormones, cell membranes, vitamins and other body substances. When an excess amount of cholesterol is present in the blood, it tends to deposit in the arteries. People with high blood cholesterol should limit their intake of cholesterol, saturated fats and overall total fat.

Because cholesterol is not found in plants, food manufacturers who advertise their vegetable oils, peanut butters or margarines as "cholesterol-free", are simply taking advantage of a characteristic that already exists in these foods.

Some Alternatives to High-Fat Products

Milk: If not chosen carefully, milk can contain large amounts of saturated fat. Homogenized milk for example, contains 3.5% fat, which means that in 1 cup (250 mL) there are 8 grams of fat. Compare that with 2% milk containing 4.7 grams of fat, 1% milk containing 2.6 grams of fat, and skim milk containing only 0.4 grams of fat per 1 cup (250 mL). Goat's milk is also very high in fat—10 grams in just 1 cup (250 mL). Soy milk is sometimes used in place of dairy milk by people who have dairy allergies. But it's missing calcium which, therefore, needs to be supplemented. Because soy milk is a non-dairy product it has no cholesterol, but 1 cup (250 mL) does contain 5 grams of fat.

Recipes in *Low-Fat Cooking* that use milk as an ingredient have been tested using skim milk. Skim evaporated milk was used in place of heavy cream for dessert toppings, or in puddings and pie fillings to give them a thick consistency. You may be surprised to know that buttermilk isn't as fattening as it sounds, and is available in 1% or 2%. It's made commercially by adding special bacteria to non-fat or low-fat milk, which gives it a slightly thicker texture and tangy flavor. Buttermilk is great in baked products, adding just a small amount of fat for flavor and tenderness.

Cheese is often a big culprit in adding fat to your diet, which is why *Low-Fat Cooking* makes use of low-fat or part-skim cheeses. In developing these recipes we reduced the amount of cheese per serving in order to lower the fat content of a recipe.

Cooking with oils/fats: When choosing a fat to use during cooking, be wary of saturated fat. The more saturated a fat, the firmer it is. Butter is harder than margarine because butter is higher in saturated fat than margarine. Instead, try margarines and oils that are highest in polyunsaturated fat and lowest in saturated fat, with a minimum ratio of 2 to 1. In *Low-Fat Cooking*, recipes that use oil are made with canola or olive oil, both of which are high in unsaturated fat and low in saturated fat. Keep in mind that all oils, whether saturated or unsaturated, contain the same amount of fat and calories—it's only the *type* of fat that is different.

The best substitution for fat when frying, sautéing or stir-frying is flavored no-stick cooking spray. These sprays use real oil with small amounts of propellants in an aerosol can, making it possible to disperse oil in a far thinner layer than would be possible with regular oil, butter or margarine. You might want to try using an olive oil, butter-flavored or garlic flavored no-stick cooking spray to enhance the flavor of your recipe.

The goal of *Low-Fat Cooking* was to lower the amount of fat in every recipe without sacrificing taste. As a result of careful testing, we determined this key guideline for you to follow when baking low-fat products: the minimum amount of fat for muffins and quick breads is 1 to 2 tbsp. (15 to 30 mL) per 1 cup (250 mL) of flour. For cakes and cookies, use a minimum of 2 tbsp. (30 mL) per 1 cup (250 mL) of flour.

Eggs: The yolk contains all the fat found in an egg, so wherever possible in *Low-Fat Cooking*, eggs have been reduced. Instead of using a whole egg, for example, some recipes will substitute 2 egg whites. Other recipes may call for an egg white substitute product (such as *Simply Egg Whites*) or egg substitute product (such as *Egg Beaters*).

1 large egg = ¼ cup (50-60 mL) egg substitute product

Egg white products work great for meringues, but whole egg substitute products do not. That's because vitamins and minerals, normally found in the removed yolks, are added back into this product. They can inhibit foaming necessary to make a meringue.

Salad dressings and mayonnaise: These two items can be very high in fat. Look for polyunsaturated oils as the first ingredient listed on the labels. The best low-fat alternative to these dressings is lemon juice or bottled dressings that contain little or no oil. Wherever possible *Low-Fat Cooking* makes use of flavor-enhancing herbs in dressings. Mustard is a great, tangy alternative to high-fat sandwich spreads.

Margarines: Tub margarines contain more water and less fat than hard margarine and butter, and it's for this reason they aren't recommended for use in baked products, or in recipes where margarine must be melted. Diet tub margarines contain even more water and should be used only as a spread for sandwiches or canapés.

What's on a Packaging Label?

Food packaging labels have valuable information, but firstly you need to understand how to read them, and secondly, how to apply the information so that you can maintain healthy eating habits.

Health messages on packaged products are required by law to emphasize the importance of the total diet and cannot exaggerate the role of one particular food or diet in disease prevention. No single product or food on its own can make a person instantly healthy, and manufacturers must be careful not to distort the roles of their products in promoting health.

Yes, but is it "light?". The word "light" on a label can mean practically anything and may have nothing to do with fat content. It could easily mean the product is light in color, light in texture, light in sugar or light in salt. Manufacturers must ensure that this confusion doesn't happen by providing sufficient information on their labels, including a statement as to why the product is "light/lite".

Less than 15% fat labels on meat products can also be confusing if you misinterpret "less than 15% fat" as meaning less than 15% of calories from fat. It could actually be as much as 70% calories from fat. Keep in mind that "less than 15% fat" refers to the amount of fat by weight of the product, not the percentage of calories from fat.

Nutrition regulations. In Canada, nutrition labeling on packaging is, at the moment, voluntary. If manufacturers decide to include a nutrition label, then they must follow specific regulations. United States manufacturers are required by law to provide accurate, easy-to-understand nutrition labels on their products. The chart (right) can help you understand how to read and use these labels properly.

CANADA

"low-fat" ("low in fat")	product contains 3 grams of fat or less per stated serving
"light in fat" ("lite in fat")	product contains 15 grams of fat or less per 100 g serving
"lower in fat than …"	product contains at least 25% less fat grams than the regular product
"reduced in fat"	product contains at least 1.5 grams less fat grams per stated serving than the regular product
"fat-free" ("contains no fat") ("very low-fat")	product contains 0.5 grams of fat or less per 100 g serving
"light" (when referring to fat) ("lite")	product is a low-fat or fat-free food, or a food containing less fat grams than the regular product
"lean" (for all ground meat and ground poultry)	contains 17% or less fat grams
"extra lean" (for all ground meat and ground poultry)	contains 10% or less fat grams
"lean" (for all other meat, poultry, fish and shellfish)	contains 10% or less fat grams
"extra lean" (for all other meat, poultry, fish and shellfish)	contains 7.5% or less fat grams

UNITED STATES

"low-fat"	product contains 3 grams of fat or less per stated serving
"fat-free"	product contains 0.5 grams of fat or less per stated serving
"reduced fat"	product contains at least 25% less fat grams when compared with a similar food
"saturated fat free"	product contains less than 0.5 grams of saturated fat per stated serving
"low saturated fat"	product contains 1 gram of saturated fat or less per stated serving and no more than 15% of calories from fat
"reduced saturated fat"	product contains at least 25% less saturated fat grams per stated serving when compared with a similar food
"light" ("lite")	product contains 50% or less grams of fat than the regular product
"lean" (for meat, poultry, fish and seafood)	contains less than 10 grams of total fat (less than 4.5 grams saturated fat, and less than 95 milligrams of cholesterol) per 100g serving
"extra lean" for meat, poultry, fish and shellfish	contains less than 5 grams of total fat (less than 2 grams saturated fat, and less than 95 milligrams cholesterol) per 100g serving

Appetizers

ven though you have chosen to eat lighter and healthier, don't forget to enjoy the good fun of nibbling before dinner! These appetizers are the ideal low-fat introduction to any meal. Be it a cocktail party, special event or just dinner at home, they can spice up a meal anytime. Whet your palate with these exciting appetizers and enjoy them with friends and family.

Mushroom Toasts

Total preparation time is 25 minutes. Garnishing with roasted peppers or pimientos will add color. Makes 28 appetizers. Pictured on page 17.

Finely chopped onion	$^3/_4$ **cup**	**175 mL**
Butter-flavored oil (such as Canola Gold)	**1 tbsp.**	**15 mL**
Finely chopped fresh mushrooms	**3 cups**	**750 mL**
All-purpose flour	**2 tsp.**	**10 mL**
Garlic powder	$^1/_4$ **tsp.**	**1 mL**
Salt	**1 tsp.**	**5 mL**
Skim evaporated milk	$^3/_4$ **cup**	**175 mL**
White wine	$^1/_4$ **cup**	**60 mL**
Bread slices	**7**	**7**
Freshly ground pepper	$^1/_2$ **tsp.**	**2 mL**
Roasted red peppers or pimiento slices, for garnish		

Sauté onion with oil in large non-stick skillet for 1 minute. Increase heat to medium-high. Add mushrooms. Sauté until liquid is evaporated. Reduce heat. ■ Stir in flour, garlic powder and salt. Slowly add milk and white wine. Boil for 2 minutes. Remove from heat. Cool to room temperature. ■ Broil one side of each bread slice on ungreased baking sheet until lightly toasted. Remove toast from oven. Spread mushroom mixture to edges of each slice, on untoasted side. Sprinkle with pepper. ■ Garnish with roasted pepper slices. Return to oven and broil until hot. Cut each toast diagonally into 4 triangles.

Nutrition Information

1 appetizer: 37 Calories; 1 g Protein; 0.6 g Total Fat (0.1 g Sat., 0.3 mg Cholesterol); 150 mg Sodium

Baked Spring Rolls

Drain the filling mixture before placing on the phyllo sheets. This will keep the pastry sheets crisp. Makes 60 spring rolls. Pictured on page 17.

Lean ground pork or chicken	**$^1/_2$ lb.**	**225 g**
Chopped onion	**1 cup**	**250 mL**
Chopped mushrooms	**2 cups**	**500 mL**
Chopped fresh bean sprouts, packed	**3 cups**	**750 mL**
Grated carrot	**1 cup**	**250 mL**
Low-sodium soy sauce	**2 tsp.**	**10 mL**
Ground turmeric	**$^1/_8$ tsp.**	**0.5 mL**
Dried crushed chilies	**$^1/_4$ tsp.**	**1 mL**
Chinese five-spice powder	**$^1/_8$ tsp.**	**0.5 mL**
Ground ginger	**$^1/_4$ tsp.**	**1 mL**
Salt	**1 tsp.**	**5 mL**
Freshly ground pepper	**$^1/_4$ tsp.**	**1 mL**
Chopped cooked shrimp	**1 cup**	**250 mL**
Toasted sesame seeds	**2 tsp.**	**10 mL**
Phyllo pastry sheets	**20**	**20**
Canola oil (or use cooking spray)	**2 tsp.**	**10 mL**

Scramble-fry pork with onion in large non-stick skillet or wok until pork is no longer pink. Drain. ■ Add mushrooms, bean sprouts and carrot. Sauté until slightly soft. Stir in next 7 ingredients. ■ Add shrimp and sesame seeds. Stir. ■ Lay single sheet of phyllo pastry on non-floured working surface. Cover remaining sheets with damp tea towel. Lightly oil surface of single pastry sheet. Cover with second sheet of phyllo pastry and lightly oil its surface as well. Cut double sheet into 6 squares. Put 1$^1/_2$ to 2 tbsp. (25 to 30 mL) filling diagonally across one-third of each square. Fold closest corner over filling. Continue to roll, tucking ends in as you go. Lay seam end down on lightly greased baking sheet. Repeat until all filling is used. Drain any liquid that accumulates in pork mixture. Lightly oil surface of spring rolls. Bake in 375°F (190°C) oven for 12 to 15 minutes until crisp and golden. Serve with Plum Sauce, page 136.

Nutrition Information

1 spring roll: 22 Calories; 1 g Protein; 1 g Total Fat (0.3 g Sat., 5.6 mg Cholesterol); 70 mg Sodium

Shrimp Salad Wraps

These can be eaten chilled, at room temperature, or even steamed over boiling water until warm.
Makes 48 salad wraps. Pictured on page 17.

Short grain white rice	$^3/_4$ cup	175 mL
Water	$1^1/_2$ cups	375 mL
Rice vinegar	1 tbsp.	15 mL
Salt	1 tsp.	5 mL
Water	$^1/_4$ cup	60 mL
Low-fat vegetable or chicken bouillon cube	$^1/_2 \times ^1/_3$ oz.	$^1/_2 \times 10.5$ g
Garlic clove, minced	1	1
Fresh medium shrimp, peeled and deveined	48	48
Curry paste (available in Oriental section of grocery store)	2 tbsp.	30 mL
Rice wrappers, $8^1/_2$ inch (21.5 cm) size	12	12
English cucumber, with peel, quartered lengthwise, and cut julienne into 2 inch (5 cm) strips	$^1/_4$	$^1/_4$
Green onions, sliced lengthwise into 2 inch (5 cm) slivers	2	2
Medium carrot, cut julienne into 2 inch (5 cm) strips	1	1
DIPPING SAUCE		
Chili sauce	$^1/_4$ cup	60 mL
Low-sodium soy sauce	2 tbsp.	30 mL
Rice vinegar	2 tbsp.	30 mL
Prepared horseradish	1 tsp.	5 mL
Liquid concentrated beef flavoring (such as Bovril)	1 tsp.	5 mL

Combine rice with first amount of water, rice vinegar and salt in medium saucepan. Bring to a boil. Cover. Simmer for 20 minutes until rice is tender. Set aside to cool. ■ Heat second amount of water and partial bouillon cube in large non-stick skillet. Cook garlic in broth until soft. Stir in shrimp. Stir-fry for 3 minutes until shrimp is cooked. Cool shrimp enough to handle. Slice in half lengthwise. Place back in skillet. Add curry paste. Stir-fry for 1 minute. ■ Soak rice wrappers, 1 at a time, in shallow pan of hot water for 1 minute until soft. Cut into quarters. Divide cucumber, carrot and onion evenly for 48 wraps. Place crosswise along wide end of quartered wrappers. Spread 1 tbsp. (15 mL) rice on top of vegetables. Top with 2 halves of shrimp. Bring two sides of wrapper over shrimp. Roll up, starting at wide end. ■ **Dipping Sauce:** Stir all 5 ingredients together in small bowl. Makes about 6 tbsp. (100 mL) sauce.

Nutrition Information

1 salad wrap with $^1/_2$ tsp. (2 mL) sauce: 31 Calories; 2 g Protein; 0.6 g Total Fat (trace Sat., 7.6 mg Cholesterol); 158 mg Sodium

Saté With Peanut Sauce

Marinades don't need oil to make meat tasty and tender. Use 16, 8 inch (20 cm) bamboo skewers, soaked in water for 10 minutes, to prevent burning when broiling kabobs. Preparing the steak when it is partially frozen will make it easier to slice. Makes 16 kabobs and 1 cup (250 mL) peanut sauce. Pictured on page 17.

Sirloin steak, 3/4-1 inch (2-2.5 cm) thick, trimmed of fat	1 lb.	454 g
INDONESIAN MARINADE		
Garlic clove, minced	1	1
Freshly minced gingerroot	1 tsp.	5 mL
Brown sugar, packed	1/3 cup	75 mL
Lemon juice, fresh or bottled	2 tbsp.	30 mL
Low-sodium soy sauce	1/2 cup	125 mL
PEANUT SAUCE		
Yogurt Cheese, page 67	1/2 cup	125 mL
Liquid honey	2 tsp.	10 mL
Dried crushed chilies	1/4 tsp.	1 mL
Lemon juice, fresh or bottled	2 tbsp.	30 mL
Smooth peanut butter	3 tbsp.	50 mL
Chili powder	1/4 tsp.	1 mL
Low-sodium soy sauce	1 tsp.	5 mL

Cut steak into long 1/8 inch (3 mm) thick slices. Put into shallow glass dish or sealable plastic bag. ■ **Indonesian Marinade:** Combine all 5 ingredients in small bowl. Pour marinade over beef. Turn to coat well. Cover or seal. Marinate beef in refrigerator for at least 30 minutes. Remove beef and discard marinade. Thread beef onto presoaked bamboo skewers. Broil 4 inches (10 cm) from heat until desired doneness or barbecue over medium-high heat for 1 1/2 minutes per side to desired doneness. ■ **Peanut Sauce:** Combine all 7 ingredients in small bowl. Refrigerate for at least 30 minutes to blend flavors. Use as dipping sauce for the beef.

Nutrition Information

1 kabob with 1 tsp. (5 mL) sauce: 76 Calories; 8 g Protein; 2.6 g Total Fat (0.7 g Sat., 13.7 mg Cholesterol); 336 mg Sodium

For a healthy low-fat snack, eat unsalted pretzels instead of salted peanuts.

Crêpe Stacks

Freeze the leftover crêpes to use for another time. Makes 2 stacks. Each stack cuts into 10 wedges. Pictured on page 17.

CRÊPE BATTER

Frozen egg product (such as Egg Beaters), thawed	$^1/_2$ cup	125 mL
Skim milk	$2^1/_4$ cups	560 mL
All-purpose flour	2 cups	500 mL
Canola oil	2 tbsp.	30 mL

SAVORY CHEESE FILLING

Non-fat spreadable herb & garlic-flavored cream cheese	8 oz.	225 g
Non-fat sour cream	$^1/_4$ cup	60 mL
Finely diced green pepper	$^1/_4$ cup	60 mL
Green onion, finely sliced	1	1
Finely diced smoked turkey, ham or beef	2 oz.	57 g

Chopped fresh parsley, for garnish

Crêpe Batter: Measure all 4 ingredients into blender. Process until smooth. Let batter stand for 1 hour to remove air bubbles. If batter seems too thick, add more skim milk, 1 tbsp. (15 mL) at a time to thin. Pour 2 tbsp. (30 mL) batter into hot crêpe pan that has been lightly greased. Swirl batter all over pan bottom. Remove crêpe when underside is lightly browned. Stack crêpes with waxed paper between each until ready to use. ■ **Savory Cheese Filling:** Combine all 5 filling ingredients in medium bowl. Mix well. Spread 2 tbsp. (30 mL) filling over each of 6 crêpes. Stack 6 crêpes, one on top of the other. ■ Garnish with sprinkle of parsley. Repeat to make 2 stacks. Chill for several hours.

Nutrition Information

1 wedge: 96 Calories; 4 g Protein; 2.5 g Total Fat (0.3 g Sat., 2.2 mg Cholesterol); 53 mg Sodium

Curried Chicken Rolls

To save time, the chicken can be cooked ahead and then reheated with 2 tbsp. (30 mL) water before adding to the tortillas. Serve with Greek Cucumber Spread, page 69. Makes 40 appetizer-size chicken rolls. Pictured on page 17.

Chili oil	1 tsp.	5 mL
Chicken fillets or boneless, skinless chicken breasts, cut lengthwise into long strips	1 lb.	454 g
Salt	$^1/_4$ tsp.	1 mL
Freshly ground pepper	$^1/_8$ tsp.	0.5 mL

(continued on next page)

Curry paste (available in Oriental section of grocery store)	1 tbsp.	15 mL
Fresh Mango Chutney, page 136	1 tbsp.	15 mL
Worcestershire sauce	1/4 tsp.	1 mL
English cucumber, with peel	1	1
Green onions, thinly sliced lengthwise	4	4
Flour tortillas, 10 inch (25 cm), warmed	4	4
Chopped fresh cilantro	2 tbsp.	30 mL

Heat oil in non-stick skillet until hot. Sprinkle chicken fillets with salt and pepper. Brown chicken in hot oil for 3 minutes, stirring often. ■ Stir in curry paste, chutney and Worcestershire sauce. Sauté for 10 minutes until chicken is no longer pink inside. ■ Slice cucumber lengthwise in half. Slice each half lengthwise into 4 strips. ■ Divide green onion, cucumber and chicken evenly and place on 1 end of each warmed tortilla. Sprinkle with cilantro. Roll up tightly. Cut into 1 inch (2.5 cm) slices. Hold together with wooden picks.

N u t r i t i o n   I n f o r m a t i o n

1 chicken roll: 33 Calories; 3 g Protein; 0.5 g Total Fat (0.1 g Sat., 6.6 mg Cholesterol); 45 mg Sodium

Pineapple Crêpe Stacks

Easy preparation and very impressive to serve to company. Makes 2 stacks. Each stack cuts into 10 wedges.

Crêpe Batter, page 14

Non-fat spreadable cream cheese	8 oz.	225 g
Non-fat sour cream	1/4 cup	60 mL
Finely diced red pepper or maraschino cherries	1/4 cup	60 mL
Icing (confectioner's) sugar	2 tsp.	10 mL
Canned crushed pineapple, drained and squeezed dry	8 oz.	227 mL

Chopped fresh parsley, for garnish

Prepare crêpe batter according to method on page 14. ■ Combine next 5 ingredients in medium bowl. Mix well. Spread 2 tbsp. (30 mL) filling over each of 6 crêpes. Stack one on top of the other. ■ Garnish with sprinkle of parsley. Repeat to make 2 stacks. Chill for several hours.

N u t r i t i o n   I n f o r m a t i o n

1 wedge: 97 Calories; 4 g Protein; 2.3 g Total Fat (0.3 g Sat., 0.7 mg Cholesterol); 29 mg Sodium

Bruschetta

Bruschetta (broo-SKEH-tah) is from the Italian word bruscare meaning "to roast over coals." Only 20 minutes preparation time. Makes 15 bruschetta.

Large plum tomatoes, seeded and diced into ¹/₂ inch (12 mm) pieces	**5-6**	**5-6**
Garlic cloves, crushed	**2**	**2**
Finely chopped fresh sweet basil	**¹/₄ cup**	**60 mL**
Olive oil	**2 tbsp.**	**30 mL**
Red wine vinegar	**2 tbsp.**	**30 mL**
Salt	**1 tsp.**	**5 mL**
Freshly ground pepper	**¹/₄ tsp.**	**1 mL**
French bread slices, 1 inch (2.5 cm) thick, lightly toasted on 1 side	**15**	**15**
Grated fresh Parmesan cheese	**2 tbsp.**	**30 mL**

Combine first 7 ingredients in medium bowl. Cover. Let stand at room temperature for at least 2 hours to allow flavors to blend. Drain. ■ Divide tomato mixture over untoasted side of each bread slice. ■ Sprinkle each with equal amount of Parmesan cheese. Place on ungreased baking sheet. Broil 6 to 8 inches (15 to 20 cm) from heat until edges are golden.

Nutrition Information

1 bruschetta: 133 Calories; 4 g Protein; 3.3 g Total Fat (0.7 g Sat., 0.7 mg Cholesterol); 405 mg Sodium

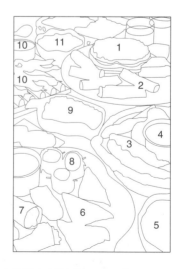

Chicken Fingers

Serve with Honey Mustard Dip, page 66, or Plum Sauce, page 136. Double the recipe if serving a larger crowd. Makes 9 chicken fingers. Pictured on page 17.

Boneless, skinless chicken breast halves, sliced into long strips, 1 inch (2.5 cm) wide	**3**	**3**
Egg whites (large), fork-beaten	**2**	**2**
Garlic powder	**³/₄ tsp.**	**4 mL**
Seasoning salt	**³/₄ tsp.**	**4 mL**
Onion powder	**³/₄ tsp.**	**4 mL**
Parsley flakes	**1 tbsp.**	**15 mL**
Corn flake crumbs	**1 cup**	**250 mL**
Cooking spray, for crispness (optional)		

Combine chicken strips with egg whites in medium bowl. Stir until chicken is coated.
■ Combine next 5 ingredients in pie plate. Dip chicken strips into crumb mixture. Coat chicken strips well. Place on lightly greased baking sheet. Lightly oil surfaces of coated chicken strips with cooking spray. Bake in 400°F (205°C) oven for 10 minutes. Turn strips over. Bake for 10 minutes until chicken is no longer pink inside and crumb coating is crisp and golden.

Nutrition Information

1 chicken finger: 93 Calories; 11 g Protein; 0.8 g Total Fat (0.2 g Sat., 22.8 mg Cholesterol); 146 mg Sodium

1. Asparagus Risotto, page 24
2. Easy Three Bean Bake, page 26
3. Spanish Rice, page 27
4. Mushroom Rice Patties, page 21
5. Rice And Barley Pilaf, page 20
6. Cornmeal Chicken With Fresh Tomato Sauce, page 93
7. Rice And Mushroom Roll-Ups, page 22

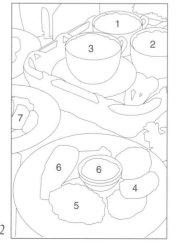

Beans & Rice

Protein and carbohydrates are just two of the healthy nutrients that come from beans and rice. Nutrition aside, they are also incredibly versatile and can make delicious side dishes and main course favorites.

Rice And Barley Pilaf

Pilaf originated in the Near East. Always begin by first browning the rice in butter or oil before cooking in the broth. Pilaf can be served as a side dish or main dish. Makes 9 cups (2.25 L). Pictured on page 18.

Butter-flavored oil (such as Canola Gold), or regular	2 tsp.	10 mL
Brown rice, uncooked	1 cup	250 mL
Pearl barley	3/4 cup	175 mL
Chopped onion	1 cup	250 mL
Chopped celery	1 cup	250 mL
Condensed chicken or beef broth	2 × 10 oz.	2 × 284 mL
Water	2 cups	500 mL
Chopped fresh parsley	2 tbsp.	30 mL
Chopped fresh sweet basil	2 tbsp.	30 mL
Freshly ground pepper	1/2 tsp.	2 mL
Medium zucchini, halved lengthwise, sliced	1	1
Medium carrots, thinly sliced	3	3
Red pepper, diced	1	1

Heat oil in large non-stick wok. Sauté rice and barley for 7 minutes until lightly browned. ■ Add onion and celery. Cook for 3 minutes. ■ Add chicken broth, water, parsley, basil and pepper. Bring to a boil. Cover and simmer for 40 minutes. ■ Add zucchini, carrot and red pepper. Stir. Cover. Cook for 35 minutes until carrot slices are tender.

Nutrition Information

1 cup (250 mL): 199 Calories; 7 g Protein; 2.7 g Total Fat (0.5 g Sat., 0.7 mg Cholesterol); 446 mg Sodium; excellent source of Fiber

Mushroom Rice Patties

These are great served for a luncheon with a salad such as Mediterranean Salad, page 130. Makes 15 patties. Pictured on page 18.

Canola oil	1 tsp.	5 mL
Finely chopped onion	1/2 cup	125 mL
Finely chopped mushrooms	1 cup	250 mL
All-purpose flour	3 tbsp.	50 mL
Garlic powder	1/8 tsp.	0.5 mL
Salt (optional)	1/2 tsp.	2 mL
Pepper	1/4 tsp.	1 mL
Cold cooked brown rice	3 cups	750 mL
Egg whites (large)	3	3
Cream of tartar	1/8 tsp.	0.5 mL
Grated low-fat medium Cheddar cheese	1 cup	250 mL

Heat oil in large non-stick skillet. Sauté onion and mushrooms until most of liquid is evaporated. ■ Add flour, garlic powder, salt and pepper. Mix well. Remove from heat. ■ Combine mushroom mixture and cold rice in large bowl. Mix well. ■ Combine egg whites with cream of tartar in medium glass bowl. Beat on high until stiff. Fold in cheese. Add to rice mixture and combine well. Lightly grease large non-stick skillet. Heat pan until hot. Use 2 to 3 tbsp. (30 to 50 mL) rice mixture for each patty. Shape into patties. Cook each side for 4 to 5 minutes until golden brown.

Nutrition Information

1 patty: 85 Calories; 4 g Protein; 2.3 g Total Fat (1.1 g Sat., 4.8 mg Cholesterol); 67 mg Sodium

....

Use non-fat or low-fat cheeses (such as part-skim mozzarella, light Parmesan cheese, 1% cottage cheese, light cream cheese or non-fat spreadable cream cheese) instead of regular cheeses.

Rice And Lentils

Long grain brown rice is used in this recipe for texture. Makes 6 cups (1.5 L).

Low-fat vegetable or chicken bouillon cubes	3 × ¹/₃ oz.	3 × 10.5 g
Boiling water	3¹/₄ cups	810 mL
Green or red lentils	1 cup	250 mL
Long grain brown rice	1 cup	250 mL
Medium onion, chopped	1	1
Dry white wine	²/₃ cup	150 mL
Garlic cloves, minced	2	2
Dried sweet basil	1 tsp.	5 mL
Dried oregano, crumbled	1 tsp.	5 mL
Ground thyme	¹/₄ tsp.	1 mL
Worcestershire sauce	1 tsp.	5 mL
Freshly ground pepper	¹/₈ tsp.	0.5 mL
Sun-dried tomato halves, chopped	5	5
Non-fat process Swiss cheese slices	8	8

Combine bouillon cubes and boiling water in large bowl. Stir until dissolved. Add next 10 ingredients. Pour into lightly greased 3 quart (3 L) casserole dish. Bake, covered, in 350°F (175°C) oven for 1¹/₂ hours, stirring every ¹/₂ hour, until rice is tender. ■ Stir in sun-dried tomato. Top with cheese slices. Bake, uncovered, for 5 minutes until cheese is melted.

Nutrition Information

1 cup (250 mL): 330 Calories; 20 g Protein; 2.5 g Total Fat (0.4 g Sat., 5.3 mg Cholesterol); 1364 mg Sodium

Rice And Mushroom Roll-Ups

Serve these with non-fat sour cream or additional sautéed onion. Makes 9 servings of 4 rolls each. Pictured on page 18.

Large Swiss or red chard leaves, halved	18	18
Large onion, chopped	1	1
Sliced mushrooms	2 cups	500 mL
Canola oil	1 tbsp.	15 mL
Condensed chicken broth	2 × 10 oz.	2 × 284 mL
Water	10 oz.	284 mL
Short grain white rice, uncooked	1¹/₄ cups	300 mL
Freshly ground pepper	¹/₄ tsp.	1 mL
Water, wine (white or red), tomato juice or apple juice	¹/₂ cup	125 mL

(continued on next page)

Lightly steam chard leaves (or drop chard leaves into boiling water for 10 seconds). Cool. Pat dry. ■ Sauté onion and mushrooms in oil until onion is soft. Add chicken broth, reserving ¹/₂ cup (125 mL) for later. Add water. Stir. Bring to a boil. ■ Add rice and pepper. Cover. Simmer for 30 to 40 minutes until rice is tender and sticky and liquid is absorbed, stirring after 15 minutes. Cool enough to handle. Place a rounded tablespoonful of rice mixture on each of the chard leaves. Roll each leaf, tucking in sides to enclose rice in chard. Arrange rolls in lightly greased 3 quart (3 L) casserole dish. ■ Pour reserved chicken broth and water over rolls. Cover. Bake in 375°F (190°C) oven for 1 hour until all liquid is absorbed and chard is tender when poked with fork.

Nutrition Information

1 serving (4 rolls): 172 Calories; 7 g Protein; 2.7 g Total Fat (0.4 g Sat., 0.7 mg Cholesterol); 642 mg Sodium

Bean Chili And Rice

Preparation time is approximately 20 minutes. This is a meal-in-one. Serves 6.

Long grain brown rice	**1¹/₂ cups**	**375 mL**
Water	**2¹/₄ cups**	**560 mL**
Salt	**1 tsp.**	**5 mL**
Finely chopped onion	**¹/₂ cup**	**125 mL**
Finely chopped celery	**¹/₂ cup**	**125 mL**
Garlic cloves, minced	**3**	**3**
Canola oil	**2 tsp.**	**10 mL**
Canned kidney beans, with liquid	**14 oz.**	**398 mL**
Canned pinto beans, with liquid	**14 oz.**	**398 mL**
Tomato sauce	**14 oz.**	**398 mL**
Chopped fresh sweet basil	**1 tbsp.**	**15 mL**
Chopped fresh parsley	**1 tbsp.**	**15 mL**
Chili powder	**1-2 tbsp.**	**15-30 mL**

Combine rice, water and salt in large covered saucepan. Bring to a boil. Simmer for 40 minutes. ■ Sauté onion, celery and garlic in oil in non-stick skillet until vegetables are tender. ■ Add remaining 6 ingredients. Stir. Simmer, covered, for 30 minutes. Add rice to chili. Stir.

Nutrition Information

1 serving: 341 Calories; 12 g Protein; 3.9 g Total Fat (0.5 g Sat., 0 mg Cholesterol); 1429 mg Sodium; excellent source of Fiber

Asparagus Risotto

The secret is in the constant stirring. Best served immediately. Makes 5 cups (1.25 L). Pictured on page 18.

Olive oil	1 tbsp.	15 mL
Chopped onion	1/2 cup	125 mL
Sliced fresh mushrooms	1 cup	250 mL
Arborio rice, uncooked	1 1/2 cups	375 mL
Grated lemon peel	2 tsp.	10 mL
Condensed chicken broth	2 × 10 oz.	2 × 284 mL
Water	1 1/2 cups	375 mL
White wine	1/2 cup	125 mL
Cut fresh asparagus, 1 inch (2.5 cm) pieces	3 cups	750 mL
Water	1/3 cup	75 mL
Chopped fresh parsley, for garnish		

Heat oil in large non-stick skillet or wok. Sauté onion and mushrooms for 5 minutes until mushroom liquid is evaporated. ■ Stir in rice and lemon peel. ■ Combine chicken broth with first amount of water and wine. Add 1/2 cup (125 mL) broth mixture to rice. Cook, stirring constantly, until broth is absorbed. Add another 2 1/2 cups (625 mL) broth mixture, 1/2 cup (125 mL) at a time. Add asparagus. Add remaining 1 1/4 cups (375 mL) broth mixture, in 2 additions. Cook, stirring constantly, until liquid is absorbed and rice is tender and creamy. ■ Add second amount of water. Remove from heat. Sprinkle with parsley. Serve immediately.

Nutrition Information

1 cup (250 mL): 335 Calories; 13 g Protein; 4.6 g Total Fat (0.9 g Sat., 1.2 mg Cholesterol); 759 mg Sodium; good source of Fiber

When the basket of rolls is put on the table, try eating them without butter or margarine; or use a diet margarine that is mostly water.

Chinese Fried Rice

The egg product tastes like the real thing, only without the cholesterol! Makes 8 cups (2 L).

Canola oil	**1 tsp.**	**5 mL**
Frozen egg product (such as Egg Beaters), thawed	**¹/₂ cup**	**125 mL**
Canola oil	**1 tsp.**	**5 mL**
Chopped onion	**1 cup**	**250 mL**
Chopped mushrooms	**1 cup**	**250 mL**
Chopped celery	**1 cup**	**250 mL**
Chopped green pepper	**1 cup**	**250 mL**
Frozen peas	**1 cup**	**250 mL**
Cold cooked long grain white rice	**4 cups**	**1 L**
Salt, to taste		
Pepper, to taste		
Low-sodium soy sauce	**3 tbsp.**	**50 mL**

Heat first amount of oil in large non-stick skillet or wok until hot. Add egg product. Cook for 2 minutes. Flip over and cook other side for 1 minute. Remove to cutting board. Slice into thin slivers. ■ Heat second amount of oil in non-stick skillet. Sauté onion, mushrooms and celery for 5 minutes until liquid from mushrooms is evaporated. ■ Add green pepper and peas. Sauté for 2 minutes until peas are just cooked. Remove vegetables to medium bowl. ■ Sauté rice in skillet for 5 minutes. Sprinkle with salt and pepper. Add egg and vegetables. ■ Slowly drizzle soy sauce over rice and vegetable mixture while sautéing.

Nutrition Information

1 cup (250 mL): 169 Calories; 7 g Protein; 2.4 g Total Fat (0.3 g Sat., 0 mg Cholesterol); 307 mg Sodium; good source of Fiber

When cooking or sautéing without butter, margarine or oil, use a lower heat setting to prevent the food from sticking or burning.

Easy Three Bean Bake

Stir the ingredients in the casserole well in order to distribute the flavors. Refrigerate any leftovers and reheat the next day. Makes 8 cups (2 L). Pictured on page 18.

Medium onion, chopped	**1**	**1**
Canned stewed tomatoes, with juice, chopped	**14 oz.**	**398 mL**
Canned white kidney beans, drained	**19 oz.**	**540 mL**
Canned pinto beans, drained	**19 oz.**	**540 mL**
Canned chick peas (garbanzo beans), drained	**19 oz.**	**540 mL**
Coarsely grated carrot	**1 cup**	**250 mL**
Garlic clove, crushed	**1**	**1**
Chopped fresh parsley	**$^1/_4$ cup**	**60 mL**
Bay leaf	**1**	**1**
Brown sugar, packed	**$^1/_4$ cup**	**60 mL**
Prepared mustard	**1 tbsp.**	**15 mL**
Worcestershire sauce	**$^1/_4$ tsp.**	**1 mL**
Salt	**$^3/_4$ tsp.**	**4 mL**
Pepper	**$^1/_4$ tsp.**	**1 mL**

Sauté onion until soft in lightly greased non-stick skillet. ■ Combine onion with remaining 13 ingredients in ungreased 3 quart (3 L) casserole dish. Cover. Bake in 325°F (160°C) oven for 1$^1/_4$ hours, removing cover for last $^1/_2$ hour of baking time.

Nutrition Information

1 cup (250 mL): 192 Calories; 9 g Protein; 1.4 g Total Fat (0.2 g Sat., 0 mg Cholesterol); 648 mg Sodium; excellent source of Fiber

· ·

tip

Serve meals that use lower portions of meat, fish or poultry and higher portions of pasta, rice and vegetables.

Spanish Rice

Preparation time is 20 minutes. Makes 4 cups (1 L). Pictured on page 18.

Condensed chicken broth	**10 oz.**	**284 mL**
Water	**¹/₂ cup**	**125 mL**
Reserved tomato juice		
Long grain brown rice, uncooked	**1 cup**	**250 mL**
Chili powder	**1 tsp.**	**5 mL**
Paprika	**1 tsp.**	**5 mL**
Dried oregano	**¹/₂ tsp.**	**2 mL**
Olive oil	**1 tsp.**	**5 mL**
Garlic cloves, crushed	**3**	**3**
Chopped onion	**¹/₂ cup**	**125 mL**
Chopped green pepper	**¹/₂ cup**	**125 mL**
Chopped celery	**¹/₂ cup**	**125 mL**
Chopped fresh sweet basil	**1 tbsp.**	**15 mL**
Canned diced tomatoes, drained, juice reserved	**14 oz.**	**398 mL**

Parsley, for garnish

Combine chicken broth, water and tomato juice in large saucepan. ■ Add rice, chili powder, paprika and oregano. Bring to a boil. Cover. Simmer for 45 minutes until rice is tender. ■ Heat oil in non-stick skillet. Sauté garlic, onion, green pepper and celery for about 5 minutes until onion is soft. ■ Add basil and tomatoes. Sauté for 5 minutes. Add to cooked rice mixture. ■ Garnish with parsley.

Nutrition Information

1 cup (250 mL): 257 Calories; 9 g Protein; 3.9 g Total Fat (0.7 g Sat., 0.8 mg Cholesterol); 662 mg Sodium; good source of Fiber

....

If you would rather not use the non-stick aerosol cooking spray, pour oil into a spray bottle and keep it in the kitchen cupboard. It's a convenient way to mist your food and baking pans with oil whenever needed.

Cakes & Pies

everyone will say "yes please!" when you offer these delicious low-fat sweets at your next dinner party. Now is the time to indulge. These wonderful pie crusts are handy to have on hand for any pie or mousse filling. Because they tend to be softer and more fragile than traditional high-fat pie crusts, it's recommended that if freezing, they be left in the pie plate.

Not Such An Angel Cake

Serve with Whipped Topping, page 57. Make sure all utensils and the springform pan are free from grease to prevent the cake from falling. Serves 12.

Egg whites, large (or 1$\frac{1}{2}$ cups, 375 mL, egg white substitute such as Simply Egg Whites)	**12**	**12**
Cream of tartar	**1 tsp.**	**5 mL**
Salt	**$\frac{1}{4}$ tsp.**	**1 mL**
Maple flavoring	**$\frac{1}{2}$ tsp.**	**2 mL**
Vanilla	**1 tsp.**	**5 mL**
Granulated sugar	**1 cup**	**250 mL**
Organic or finely milled whole wheat flour	**1 cup**	**250 mL**
Icing (confectioner's) sugar	**$\frac{3}{4}$ cup**	**175 mL**

Beat egg whites with cream of tartar and salt until soft peaks form. ■ Add maple flavoring and vanilla. Gradually add granulated sugar, 1 tbsp. (15 mL) at a time, beating until all sugar is used and stiff peaks form. ■ Sift flour and icing sugar together twice. Fold about $\frac{1}{4}$ flour mixture gently into egg whites with rubber spatula. Fold in remaining flour until incorporated into egg whites. Pour batter into ungreased 10 inch (25 cm) springform pan. Bake in 325°F (160°C) oven for 45 minutes until wooden pick inserted in center comes out clean. Remove from oven and immediately invert pan to cool.

Nutrition Information

1 serving: 151 Calories; 5 g Protein; 0.2 g Total Fat (trace Sat., 0 mg Cholesterol); 142 mg Sodium

Fresh Strawberry Pie

Raspberry-flavored gelatin and fresh raspberries can also be used instead of strawberries to make a fresh raspberry pie. Cuts into 8 pieces.

Granulated sugar	$^3/_4$ cup	175 mL
Cornstarch	2 tbsp.	30 mL
Water	$1^1/_2$ cups	375 mL
Strawberry-flavored gelatin (jelly powder)	1 × 3 oz.	1 × 85 g
Sliced fresh strawberries	3 cups	750 mL
Graham Crust, page 32	1	1
Envelope dessert topping (such as Dream Whip)	1	1
Skim milk	$^1/_2$ cup	125 mL
Vanilla flavoring	1 tsp.	5 mL

Sliced fresh strawberries, for garnish

Combine sugar and cornstarch in medium saucepan. Gradually stir in water. Heat on high until boiling. Boil for 2 minutes. Add gelatin. Stir until dissolved. Cool slightly on counter. Add strawberries to gelatin mixture. ■ Pour into crust. Lay plastic wrap directly on surface of pie. Refrigerate until cold and set. ■ Beat dessert topping and skim milk together according to package directions. Add vanilla flavoring. Beat until stiff. Pipe onto cooled pie. ■ Garnish with strawberries.

Nutrition Information

1 piece: 295 Calories; 4 g Protein; 8.3 g Total Fat (3.2 g Sat., 0.3 mg Cholesterol); 286 mg Sodium

Chocolate Angel Food Cake

Using a commercial cake mix results in a preparation time of only 10 minutes. Serves 12.

Package white angel food cake mix	1	1
Cocoa	2 tbsp.	30 mL

Combine dry cake mix with cocoa. Prepare and bake cake according to package directions.

Nutrition Information

1 serving: 165 Calories; 4 g Protein; 0.2 g Total Fat (trace g Sat., 0 mg Cholesterol); 81 mg Sodium

Rich Burnt Sugar Cake

You will never believe this is low-fat. Total preparation time is 45 minutes. Serves 12. Pictured on page 35.

Cake flour	2 cups	500 mL
Baking powder	1¼ tsp.	6 mL
Baking soda	1¼ tsp.	6 mL
Salt	½ tsp.	2 mL
Butter-flavored oil (such as Canola Gold)	¼ cup	60 mL
Brown sugar, packed	⅔ cup	150 mL
Vanilla	1½ tsp.	7 mL
Canned pears, drained and puréed	14 oz.	398 mL
1% buttermilk	⅔ cup	150 mL
Egg whites (large)	4	4
Cream of tartar	½ tsp.	2 mL
Brown sugar, packed	⅔ cup	150 mL
BURNT SUGAR SAUCE		
Granulated sugar	1¼ cups	300 mL
Skim evaporated milk	¾ cup	175 mL
Finely crushed toasted pecans	1 tbsp.	15 mL

Sift flour, baking powder, baking soda and salt together in medium bowl. ■ Beat oil with first amount of brown sugar, vanilla and pears in large bowl. Add flour mixture in 3 parts alternately with buttermilk in 2 parts, beginning and ending with flour mixture. Combine well after each addition. ■ Beat egg whites with cream of tartar in large bowl until soft peaks form. Gradually beat in second amount of brown sugar until stiff peaks form. Fold egg white mixture, ⅓ at a time, into flour mixture. Pour into lightly greased 10 inch (25 cm) springform pan. Bake in 350°F (175°C) oven for 40 minutes until wooden pick inserted in center comes out clean. Cool for 10 minutes.
■ **Burnt Sugar Sauce:** Melt sugar in cast-iron frying pan on medium. Cook, stirring constantly, for 8 to 10 minutes. Hard lumps will form during cooking time but will eventually melt. Reduce heat. Gradually add evaporated milk, stirring constantly. Stir until a smooth, thick, deep golden brown syrup forms. Makes 1⅓ cups (325 mL) sauce.
■ Run knife around outside edge of cake. Remove springform pan sides. Carefully slide knife between bottom of pan and cake. Remove cake, right side up, onto large plate. Poke holes, 1½ inches (3.8 cm) apart, into top of cake with skewer or large meat fork. Pour warm Burnt Sugar Sauce over top of cake. Sprinkle with pecans.

N u t r i t i o n   I n f o r m a t i o n

1 serving: 334 Calories; 5 g Protein; 5.5 g Total Fat (0.5 g Sat., 1.1 mg Cholesterol); 334 mg Sodium

Vanilla Wafer Crust

Preparation time is only 10 minutes. Serve Banana Butterscotch Cream Pie, page 37, in this crust. Makes 1 single pie crust, enough for 8 servings. Pictured on page 35.

Vanilla wafer crumbs	**1¹/₂ cups**	**375 mL**
Hard margarine, melted	**2 tbsp.**	**30 mL**

Combine wafer crumbs and margarine in small bowl. Reserve 2 tbsp. (30 mL) crumb mixture for topping. Press remaining crumb mixture into lightly greased 9 inch (22 cm) pie plate. Bake in 350°F (175°C) oven for 10 minutes. Cool slightly before filling.

Nutrition Information

¹/₈ crust: 135 Calories; 1 g Protein; 6.5 g Total Fat (1.5 g Sat., 14.9 mg Cholesterol); 92 mg Sodium

Corn Flake Crust

Use this crust in a springform pan or pie plate with a cream cheese type filling. Then bake. Makes 1 single pie crust, enough for 8 servings.

Corn flake crumbs	**2 cups**	**500 mL**
Granulated sugar	**1 tbsp.**	**15 mL**
Hard margarine, softened	**1 tbsp.**	**15 mL**
Water	**2 tsp.**	**10 mL**

Combine crumbs, sugar and margarine in food processor. Process until well mixed. ■ Add 1 tsp. (5 mL) water. Process. Add remaining 1 tsp. (5 mL) water. Process again. Press into lightly greased 9 inch (22 cm) pie plate. Bake in 350°F (175°C) oven for 10 minutes. Cool slightly before filling.

Nutrition Information

¹/₈ crust: 111 Calories; 2 g Protein; 1.5 g Total Fat (0.3 g Sat., 0 mg Cholesterol); 260 mg Sodium

· ·

Use an egg substitute (such as Egg Beaters), or use two egg whites in place of one whole egg. One large egg contains 5 grams of fat; ¹/₄ cup (60 mL) Egg Beaters contains only 0.4 grams of fat; egg whites do not contain any fat.

Apricot Cheese Pie

Preparation time is 30 minutes. Similar in texture to cheesecake. Cuts into 8 pieces. Pictured on page 35.

Dried apricots	**12**	**12**
Apricot nectar	**1/2 cup**	**125 mL**
Granulated sugar	**1/4 cup**	**60 mL**
Light cream cheese, softened	**4 oz.**	**125 g**
Granulated sugar	**3/4 cup**	**175 mL**
Yogurt Cheese, page 67	**2 cups**	**500 mL**
All-purpose flour	**2 tbsp.**	**30 mL**
Vanilla	**1 tsp.**	**5 mL**
Frozen egg product (such as Egg Beaters), thawed	**1/2 cup**	**125 mL**
Corn Flake Crust, page 31, or Graham Crust, below, unbaked	**1**	**1**
Low-fat frozen whipped topping (such as Light Cool Whip), thawed, for garnish	**2 cups**	**500 mL**

Combine apricots, nectar and sugar in small saucepan. Cover. Simmer for 10 to 15 minutes until soft. Let cool. Place in blender. Process until smooth. ■ Beat cream cheese and sugar together on low in large bowl until smooth. ■ Add yogurt cheese, flour, vanilla, egg product and apricot mixture. Beat until smooth. ■ Pour into unbaked pie shell. Bake in 325°F (160°C) oven for 50 minutes until almost set in middle. Turn oven off. Let stand in oven for 10 minutes. Remove to wire rack to cool. ■ Garnish with whipped topping.

Nutrition Information

1 piece: 350 Calories; 12 g Protein; 4.4 g Total Fat (1.8 g Sat., 10.2 mg Cholesterol); 533 mg Sodium

Graham Crust

Use this as a base for pies or desserts. So simple and quick. Makes 1 single crust, enough for 8 servings. Pictured on page 35.

Graham wafer crumbs	**1 1/2 cups**	**375 mL**
Diet tub margarine, melted	**1/3 cup**	**75 mL**

Mix graham crumbs and margarine in small bowl. Pack crumb mixture evenly and firmly on bottom and up sides of ungreased 10 inch (25 cm) pie plate. Bake for 10 minutes in 350°F (175°C) oven. Cool.

Nutrition Information

1/8 crust: 117 Calories; 2 g Protein; 5.9 g Total Fat (1.2 g Sat., 0 mg Cholesterol); 145 mg Sodium

Fresh Lemon Poppy Seed Cake

Fresh lemons are the secret to this cake's success. You will need two medium-sized lemons for this recipe. Serves 12. Pictured on page 35 and on the back cover.

All-purpose flour	**2^1/$_2$ cups**	**625 mL**
Baking soda	**1 tsp.**	**5 mL**
Poppy seeds	**^{1}/$_4$ cup**	**60 mL**
Salt	**^{1}/$_2$ tsp.**	**2 mL**
Hard margarine, softened	**^{1}/$_4$ cup**	**60 mL**
Grated lemon peel	**2 tbsp.**	**30 mL**
Applesauce	**^{1}/$_4$ cup**	**60 mL**
Granulated sugar	**1^1/$_2$ cups**	**375 mL**
Large egg	**1**	**1**
Egg whites (large)	**4**	**4**
1% buttermilk	**1 cup**	**250 mL**
Freshly squeezed lemon juice	**2 tbsp.**	**30 mL**
LEMON GLAZE		
Freshly squeezed lemon juice	**^{1}/$_4$ cup**	**60 mL**
Icing (confectioner's) sugar	**1^1/$_2$ cups**	**375 mL**
Strips of lemon zest, for garnish		

Combine flour, baking soda, poppy seeds and salt in small bowl. ■ Beat margarine, grated lemon peel, applesauce and sugar together in separate bowl until fluffy. Beat in egg and egg whites on high. ■ Combine buttermilk and first amount of lemon juice in large bowl. Slowly beat flour mixture into egg mixture in 3 parts, alternately with buttermilk mixture in 2 parts, beginning and ending with flour mixture. Lightly grease 12 cup (2.7 L) bundt pan. Coat with flour. Pour batter into pan. Bake in 325°F (160°C) oven for 55 minutes until wooden pick inserted in center comes out clean. Do not overbake. ■ **Lemon Glaze:** Combine lemon juice with icing sugar in small bowl. Mix until dissolved. Poke holes into cake with long-tined fork. Pour ^{1}/$_2$ lemon glaze over warm cake. Cool in pan for 30 minutes. Invert cake onto plate. Thicken remaining lemon glaze with another 1 cup (250 mL) or more icing sugar to make thicker glaze that can be drizzled over top of cooled cake. ■ Garnish with strips of zest.

Nutrition Information

1 serving: 336 Calories; 6 g Protein; 6 g Total Fat (1.2 g Sat., 18.7 mg Cholesterol); 502 mg Sodium

Homemade Chocolate Angel Food Cake

This cake does not contain any egg yolks or other fat. Sifting the flour gives this cake its light and airy texture. Serve with Whipped Topping, page 57. Serves 12. Pictured on page 35.

All-purpose flour	$^2/_3$ **cup**	**150 mL**
Granulated sugar	$^1/_4$ **cup**	**60 mL**
Cocoa	$^1/_3$ **cup**	**75 mL**
Egg whites, large (or 1$^1/_2$ cups, 375 mL, egg white product such as Simply Egg Whites)	**12**	**12**
Cream of tartar	**1 tsp.**	**5 mL**
Vanilla	**1 tsp.**	**5 mL**
Salt, sprinkle		
Granulated sugar	**1 cup**	**250 mL**

Sift flour, first amount of sugar and cocoa together twice into medium bowl. Set aside. ■ Beat egg whites with cream of tartar, vanilla and salt until foamy. Gradually beat in second amount of sugar until stiff peaks form. Sift $^1/_4$ flour mixture over egg white mixture. Fold in gently just until flour mixture disappears. Repeat 3 more times. Pour into ungreased 10 inch (25 cm) tube pan. Run knife through batter to remove any air pockets. Bake in 350°F (175°C) oven for 50 minutes until cake springs back when gently touched. Invert pan onto counter to cool.

Nutrition Information

1 serving: 134 Calories; 5 g Protein; 0.3 g Total Fat (0.1 g Sat., 0 mg Cholesterol); 85 mg Sodium

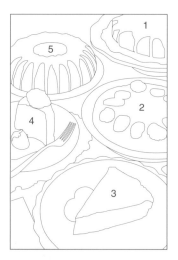

Banana Butterscotch Cream Pie

Preparation and baking time will take only 30 minutes in total. Cuts into 8 pieces. Pictured on page 35.

Brown sugar, packed	1/4 **cup**	**60 mL**
All-purpose flour	**2 tbsp.**	**30 mL**
Cornstarch	**2 tbsp.**	**30 mL**
Salt	1/2 **tsp.**	**2 mL**
Skim milk	**1 cup**	**250 mL**
Skim evaporated milk	**1 cup**	**250 mL**
Frozen egg product (such as Egg Beaters), thawed	1/3 **cup**	**75 mL**
Vanilla	**1 tsp.**	**5 mL**
Butterscotch flavoring	**1 tsp.**	**5 mL**
Medium bananas, sliced	**2**	**2**
Vanilla Wafer Crust, page 31	**1**	**1**

**Low-fat frozen whipped topping (such as
  Light Cool Whip), thawed, for garnish**
Sliced bananas, for garnish

Stir brown sugar, flour, cornstarch and salt together in medium saucepan. Slowly whisk in skim milk and evaporated milk. Heat on medium until boiling and thickened. Remove from heat. Gradually whisk in egg product. Heat on low for 2 minutes. Remove from heat. Add vanilla and butterscotch flavorings. ■ Gently stir in sliced bananas. ■ Pour filling into crust. Sprinkle with reserved crumb mixture. Lay plastic wrap directly on filling. Refrigerate until cold. ■ Garnish with whipped topping and bananas.

Nutrition Information

1 piece: 249 Calories; 7 g Protein; 6.9 g Total Fat (1.7 g Sat., 16.7 mg Cholesterol);
  340 mg Sodium

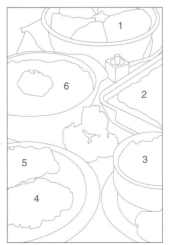

1. Chicken Pot Pie, page 42
2. Vegetable Layered Polenta, page 104
3. Chicken Fagioli Stew, page 41
4. Mardi Gras Pilaf, page 40
5. Tangy Broccoli Salad, page 119
6. Sassy Chicken Casserole, page 40

Casseroles & Stews

All-in-one casseroles and stews can be so convenient and tasty, and now, even low-fat! This exciting selection features new and traditional recipes that have been converted into delicious, low-fat dishes.

Delish Fish Casserole

A delicate balance between the tomato and the fish flavors. Serves 4.

Stewed tomatoes, with juice, chopped	**28 oz.**	**796 mL**
Granulated sugar	**1 tsp.**	**5 mL**
Worcestershire sauce	**2 tsp.**	**10 mL**
Salt	**$^1/_8$ tsp.**	**0.5 mL**
Finely chopped onion	**$^1/_4$ cup**	**60 mL**
Boneless cod fillets, cut into bite-size chunks	**1 lb.**	**454 g**
Whole fresh bread slices, processed into bread crumbs	**3**	**3**
Hard margarine, melted	**2 tbsp.**	**30 mL**

Combine first 5 ingredients in medium saucepan. Bring to a boil. Reduce heat. Simmer, uncovered, for 30 minutes until thickened and reduced. ■ Place cod in single layer on bottom of ungreased 2 quart (2 L) casserole dish. Pour tomato mixture over cod. ■ Combine bread crumbs with margarine. Mix well. Sprinkle over surface of casserole. Bake in 375°F (190°C) oven for 20 minutes until topping is golden and fish flakes easily with fork.

Nutrition Information

1 serving: 263 Calories; 24 g Protein; 7.1 g Total Fat (1.5 g Sat., 49.4 mg Cholesterol); 895 mg Sodium

Turkey Stew With Sweet Potatoes

This is easy to make ahead and can be refrigerated or frozen. Serves 6 to 8.

Boneless, skinless turkey breast	1¹/₂ lbs.	680 g
Leeks, sliced	2	2
Large celery stalks, sliced ¹/₂ inch (12 mm) thick	2	2
Garlic clove, minced	1	1
Chicken bouillon powder	³/₄ tsp.	4 mL
Boiling water	³/₄ cup	175 mL
Cornstarch	2 tbsp.	30 mL
Gravy browner	1 tsp.	5 mL
White wine	¹/₂ cup	125 mL
Bay leaves	2	2
Ground thyme	¹/₂ tsp.	2 mL
Ground oregano	¹/₂ tsp.	2 mL
Salt	¹/₄ tsp.	1 mL
Pepper	¹/₄ tsp.	1 mL
Frozen peas, thawed	1 cup	250 mL
Frozen corn, thawed	1 cup	250 mL
Cooked and mashed sweet potato	3 cups	750 mL
Brown sugar, packed (optional)	¹/₄ cup	60 mL
Large egg, fork-beaten	1	1
Salt	¹/₄ tsp.	1 mL
Pepper	¹/₄ tsp.	1 mL
Hard margarine, melted (or use cooking spray)	2 tsp.	10 mL

Cut turkey breast into ³/₄ inch (2 cm) pieces or cubes. Lightly grease non-stick wok or frying pan and heat over medium-high until hot. Add turkey and sauté until lightly browned. Remove turkey to ungreased 2 quart (2 L) casserole dish. In same frying pan, toss in leeks, celery and garlic. Stir-fry for 3 minutes. Spoon vegetables over turkey. ■ Dissolve bouillon powder in boiling water in small bowl. Add cornstarch, gravy browner and wine. Mix well. Pour over turkey. Add bay leaves, thyme, oregano, salt and pepper. Stir. Bake, covered, in 350°F (175°C) oven for 45 minutes. Add peas and corn. Stir. Bake, covered, for 15 minutes until peas and corn are hot. ■ Combine sweet potato with brown sugar, egg, salt and pepper until smooth. Spread over casserole, or pipe in lattice design. Dab surface with margarine and bake, uncovered, for about 20 minutes until lightly browned and hot.

Nutrition Information

¹/₆ recipe: 433 Calories; 35 g Protein; 3.9 g Total Fat (1 g Sat., 106 mg Cholesterol); 488 mg Sodium

Sassy Chicken Casserole

Using Mexican-style stewed tomatoes and jalapeños gives this dish some extra zip. Serves 6. Pictured on page 36.

Long grain white rice, uncooked	1¹/₂ cups	375 mL
Canned Mexican-style stewed tomatoes, with juice, chopped or broken up	2 × 14 oz.	2 × 398 mL
Garlic cloves, crushed	2	2
Medium onion, chopped	1	1
Jalapeño pepper, finely diced (optional)	1	1
Chili powder	1 tsp.	5 mL
Water	1¹/₂ cups	375 mL
Skinless, boneless chicken pieces, visible fat removed	2 lbs.	900 g
Chopped fresh cilantro or parsley, for garnish		

Place rice in bottom of lightly greased 3 quart (3 L) casserole dish. ■ Combine tomatoes, garlic, onion, jalapeño pepper, chili powder and water in medium bowl. Stir well. Pour ¹/₂ mixture over rice. Arrange chicken pieces on top of tomato layer and top with remaining tomato mixture. Bake, covered, in 325°F (160°C) oven for 1¹/₂ hours until chicken is cooked and all liquid is absorbed. ■ Garnish with cilantro.

Nutrition Information

1 serving: 311 Calories; 21 g Protein; 2.7 g Total Fat (0.6 g Sat., 49.7mg Cholesterol); 428 mg Sodium

Mardi Gras Pilaf

Attractive contrast of dark and light colors. Only 20 minutes preparation time. Serves 6. Pictured on page 36.

Olive oil	1 tsp.	5 mL
Boneless, skinless chicken breast halves, cut into slices	3	3
Medium onion, coarsely chopped	1	1
Large green pepper, chopped	1	1
Garlic cloves, crushed	2	2
Canned black beans, drained and rinsed	19 oz.	540 mL
Canned diced tomatoes, with juice	14 oz.	398 mL
Salsa, medium or hot	1 cup	250 mL
Water	1 cup	250 mL
Short grain white rice, uncooked	1 cup	250 mL
Ground cumin	¹/₄ tsp.	1 mL
Ground turmeric	¹/₂ tsp.	2 mL
Ground cinnamon	¹/₄ tsp.	1 mL
Salt	¹/₄ tsp.	1 mL

(continued on next page)

Heat oil in non-stick skillet. Add chicken, onion, green pepper and garlic. Stir-fry for about 5 minutes until chicken starts to brown. ■ Add remaining 9 ingredients. Bring to a boil. Simmer, covered, for about 20 minutes, stirring occasionally, until rice is tender and chicken is cooked.

Nutrition Information

1 serving: 306 Calories; 22 g Protein; 2.2 g Total Fat (0.4 g Sat., 34.2 mg Cholesterol); 1016 mg Sodium

Chicken Fagioli Stew

Fagioli (fa-ZHOH-lee) is the Italian word for beans. Serve in shallow bowls with fresh crusty bread. Serves 6. Pictured on page 36.

Boneless, skinless chicken breast halves	**4**	**4**
Low-fat Italian dressing	**$^1/_4$ cup**	**60 mL**
Large onion, coarsely chopped	**1**	**1**
Garlic clove, crushed	**1**	**1**
Sliced celery, $^1/_4$ inch (6 mm) pieces	**1 cup**	**250 mL**
Sliced carrot, $^1/_4$ inch (6 mm) coins	**1 cup**	**250 mL**
Medium potatoes, peeled and cut into $1^1/_2$ inch (4 cm) cubes	**3**	**3**
Condensed chicken broth	**10 oz.**	**284 mL**
Dried rosemary, crushed (or use 1 fresh sprig)	**1 tsp.**	**5 mL**
Chopped fresh sweet basil	**$^1/_4$ cup**	**60 ml**
Sun-dried tomato halves, softened in boiling water for 10 minutes, finely chopped	**6**	**6**
Canned cannellini beans (white kidney beans), drained	**19 oz.**	**540 mL**

Cut chicken breasts into 1 inch (2.5 cm) chunks. Combine with dressing in medium bowl. Let stand while preparing vegetables. ■ Lightly grease non-stick skillet or wok. Sauté onion and garlic for 2 minutes. Add chicken with dressing. Sauté for 5 minutes. ■ Add celery, carrot, potato, broth, rosemary, basil and tomato. Reduce heat. Simmer, covered, for 40 minutes until vegetables are tender. Stir in beans. Simmer, uncovered, until hot.

Nutrition Information

1 serving: 215 Calories; 26 g Protein; 2.5 g Total Fat (0.6 g Sat., 46.8 mg Cholesterol); 653 mg Sodium

Chicken Pot Pie

The same home-spun taste of traditional chicken pot pie but with less fat! Serves 6. Pictured on page 36.

Boneless, skinless chicken breast halves, cut into 1 inch (2.5 cm) pieces	**6**	**6**
Large onion, chopped	**1**	**1**
Clove garlic, crushed	**1**	**1**
Sliced fresh mushrooms	**1 cup**	**250 mL**
Thinly sliced carrot	**2 cups**	**500 mL**
Sliced celery	**1¹/₂ cups**	**375 mL**
Ground sage	**¹/₈ tsp.**	**0.5 mL**
Ground thyme	**¹/₈ tsp.**	**0.5 mL**
Freshly ground pepper	**¹/₂ tsp.**	**2 mL**
Condensed chicken broth	**10 oz.**	**284 mL**
Skim evaporated milk	**13¹/₂ oz.**	**385 mL**
All-purpose flour	**¹/₃ cup**	**75 mL**
CRUST		
All-purpose flour	**²/₃ cup**	**150 mL**
Whole wheat flour	**¹/₂ cup**	**125 mL**
Baking powder	**1 tbsp.**	**15 mL**
Salt	**¹/₂ tsp.**	**2 mL**
Granulated sugar	**¹/₂ tsp.**	**2 mL**
Olive oil or canola oil	**2¹/₂ tbsp.**	**37 mL**
Skim milk	**¹/₂ cup**	**125 mL**

Lightly grease non-stick skillet or wok and heat on medium-high until hot. Add ¹/₂ chicken pieces, searing until chicken just starts to brown. Remove with slotted spoon to lightly greased 3 quart (3 L) casserole dish. Repeat with remaining chicken. ■ In same skillet, sauté onion, garlic and mushrooms until onion is soft. Add carrot, celery, sage, thyme and pepper. Stir-fry for 2 minutes. Pour in chicken broth. Bring to a boil. Reduce heat. Simmer, covered, for 20 minutes, until carrot is tender. ■ Combine evaporated milk and flour in shaker or jar until smooth. Pour slowly into skillet, stirring until mixture boils and thickens. Pour over chicken. Stir to combine. ■ **Crust:** Combine all 5 dry ingredients in medium bowl. Stir in oil until well mixed. Stir in milk with fork until all flour is combined. Knead dough 8 to 10 times on floured surface. Pat or roll out to shape of top of casserole dish. Cut dough into wedges or squares and lay pieces on top of casserole. Bake, uncovered, in 425°F (220°C) oven for 20 to 25 minutes until bubbling and crust is lightly browned on top.

Nutrition Information

1 serving: 405 Calories; 40 g Protein; 8.5 g Total Fat (1.5 g Sat., 71 mg Cholesterol); 760 mg Sodium

Beef Pot Pie

Using phyllo pastry takes a little extra time, but it is certainly worth it. Serves 6 to 8.

Lean top sirloin, cut into $1/2$ inch (12 mm) cubes	1 lb.	454 g
Condensed beef broth (10 oz., 284 mL), plus water to make	2 cups	500 mL
Sliced carrot, $1/2$ inch (12 mm) thick	$1^1/_2$ cups	375 mL
Diced turnip, cut into $1/2$ inch (12 mm) cubes	$1^1/_2$ cups	375 mL
Large onion, cut into large wedges, lengthwise	1	1
Diced red potato, with peel	$1^1/_2$ cups	375 mL
Ground marjoram	$1/4$ tsp.	1 mL
Dried thyme	$1/2$ tsp.	2 mL
Dried oregano	$1/2$ tsp.	2 mL
Salt	$1/2$ tsp.	2 mL
All-purpose flour	$1/3$ cup	75 mL
Skim evaporated milk	$1/2$ cup	125 mL
Frozen peas	1 cup	250 mL
Phyllo dough sheets, thawed	2	2
Hard margarine, melted (or use cooking spray)	2 tsp.	10 mL
Fine dry bread crumbs	2 tbsp.	30 mL

Cover beef cubes with beef broth in large saucepan or Dutch oven. Bring to a boil. Reduce heat. Simmer, covered, for 15 minutes. Stir in carrot and turnip. Cover. Simmer for 10 minutes. Add onion, potato, marjoram, thyme, oregano and salt. Cover. Simmer until vegetables are tender. ■ Combine flour and milk with small whisk until smooth. Stir into stew and cook until thickened. Stir in peas. Heat until stew is hot. Pour into ungreased 3 quart (3 L) casserole dish. ■ Lay out 1 large sheet of phyllo dough. Brush surface with 1 tsp. (5 mL) margarine and sprinkle lightly with $1/2$ bread crumbs. Cover with second sheet. Brush lightly with remaining 1 tsp. (5 mL) margarine and sprinkle with remaining crumbs. Cut in half, crosswise and stack. Cut into 1 inch (2.5 cm) strips. Weave in lattice or lay diagonally over stew. Trim ends and tuck underneath. Bake in 375°F (190°C) oven for 25 to 30 minutes until golden and hot.

Nutrition Information

$1/6$ recipe: 254 Calories; 22 g Protein; 5 g Total Fat (1.7 g Sat., 36.5 mg Cholesterol); 709 mg Sodium

Riviera Chicken Casserole

To get 3 cups (750 mL) chopped cooked chicken, start with 3 whole medium chicken breasts (about 1¹/₄ lbs., 560 g). Cover and simmer in a skillet with about 1 cup (250 mL) water for 12 to 14 minutes until no longer pink. Serves 6.

Rotini or other spiral pasta	**2 cups**	**500 mL**
Boiling water	**8 cups**	**2 L**
Salt (optional)	**1 tsp.**	**5 mL**
Thinly sliced leek, white part only	**1³/₄ cups**	**425 mL**
Sliced fresh mushrooms	**3 cups**	**750 mL**
Condensed chicken broth	**10 oz.**	**284 mL**
White wine	**¹/₂ cup**	**125 mL**
Cornstarch	**2 tbsp.**	**30 mL**
Water	**¹/₂ cup**	**125 mL**
Grated low-fat Swiss cheese	**¹/₂ cup**	**125 mL**
Chopped cooked chicken	**3 cups**	**750 mL**
Canned artichoke hearts, drained and chopped	**14 oz.**	**398 mL**
Sun-dried tomato halves, softened in boiling water for 10 minutes, finely chopped	**4**	**4**
Chopped fresh parsley (optional)	**¹/₄ cup**	**60 mL**

Cook pasta in boiling water and salt in large uncovered Dutch oven for 7 to 9 minutes until tender but firm. Drain. Rinse. Drain again. Set aside. ■ Lightly grease large non-stick skillet or wok. Sauté leek and mushrooms until all liquid has evaporated. Pour in broth and wine. Combine cornstarch and water in small cup and pour into broth mixture. Bring to a boil, stirring until thickened. Remove from heat. ■ Stir in cheese, chicken, artichoke hearts, tomatoes and pasta. Pour into lightly greased 2 quart (2 L) casserole dish. Bake in 375°F (190°C) oven for 30 minutes until hot and bubbling. ■ Sprinkle with parsley.

Nutrition Information

1 serving: 359 Calories; 35 g Protein; 6.1 g Total Fat (2.3 g Sat., 70.2 mg Cholesterol); 566 mg Sodium

Variation: For a different flavor, stir 2 tbsp. (30 mL) chopped fresh sweet basil and 1 tbsp. (15 mL) granulated sugar into casserole before baking.

Desserts

here is always room for dessert—especially when they're low in fat! Tantalize your taste

buds with this irresistible selection—you won't feel guilty indulging when you find

out how low in fat they really are.

Latté Cake Roll

Double the filling if you want to fill and ice two rolls, or freeze one of the rolls for another day! One roll cuts into 12 slices. Pictured on page 53.

White angel food cake commercial mix, unbaked	1	1
Cocoa	1 tbsp.	15 mL
Cold strong prepared coffee	1$^1/_3$ cups	325 mL
Icing (confectioner's) sugar, sprinkle		
LATTÉ FILLING (for 1 roll)		
Envelopes dessert topping (such as Dream Whip)	2	2
Cold strong prepared coffee	1 cup	250 mL
Chocolate flavoring	2 tsp.	10 mL
Chocolate sprinkles, for garnish	1 tbsp.	15 mL

Prepare angel food cake according to package directions, adding cocoa and substituting first amount of coffee for water. Line 2, 10 × 15 inch (25 × 38 cm) jelly roll pans with waxed paper. Pour cake mixture evenly into pans. Bake in 400°F (205°C) oven for 8 to 10 minutes. Immediately turn both out onto large tea towels that have been sprinkled with icing sugar. Remove waxed paper. Roll up cake from short side, using tea towel to help roll. Set aside to cool. ■ **Latté Filling:** Combine dessert topping, second amount of coffee and chocolate flavoring in chilled bowl. Beat on high until stiff. ■ Unroll 1 cooled cake. Spread with $^1/_2$ filling. Roll up gently. Place on platter. Ice with remaining filling. Garnish with chocolate sprinkles. Unroll second cake. Lay waxed paper on the inside. Roll up. Cover with plastic wrap. Freeze in large freezer bag.

Nutrition Information

1 slice: 191 Calories; 5 g Protein; 3.3 g Total Fat (2.8 g Sat., trace Cholesterol); 96 mg Sodium

Chocolate Decadence

Use a sharp knife when cutting this extraordinary dessert. Wipe knife clean between cuts. Serve with fresh raspberries or raspberry sauce. Cuts into 10 wedges.

Granulated sugar	**³/₄ cup**	**175 mL**
Cocoa	**¹/₂ cup**	**125 mL**
All-purpose flour	**¹/₃ cup**	**75 mL**
Skim evaporated milk	**²/₃ cup**	**150 mL**
Chocolate chips	**³/₄ cup**	**175 mL**
Strained prunes (baby food)	**¹/₃ cup**	**75 mL**
Large eggs	**3**	**3**
Granulated sugar	**¹/₄ cup**	**60 mL**

**Icing (confectioner's) sugar or cocoa (optional),
    for garnish**
**Low-fat frozen whipped topping (such as Light
    Cool Whip), for garnish**

Combine first amount of sugar, cocoa and flour in medium saucepan. Slowly add evaporated milk, whisking until smooth. Heat gently, while stirring, until very warm. Do not boil. Remove from heat. ■ Stir in chocolate chips until melted. Add prunes. Stir together. ■ Beat eggs together for 3 to 4 minutes until frothy and thickened. Gradually add second amount of sugar. Gently fold in chocolate mixture. Pour into lightly greased 10 inch (25 cm) springform pan. Bake in 350°F (175°C) oven for 35 minutes until wooden pick inserted in center has some crumbs sticking to it. Do not overbake. It will be quite moist. Cool. ■ Dust with icing sugar. Garnish with whipped topping.

Nutrition Information

1 wedge: 217 Calories; 5 g Protein; 6.5 g Total Fat (3.5 g Sat., 52.6 mg Cholesterol);
    40 mg Sodium

· ·

Instead of high-fat dessert, choose low-fat angel food cake or meringue.

Biscotti is an Italian biscuit that has been baked twice. It's made by first forming the dough into a loaf and baking it, then slicing the loaf into long, narrow pieces and baking again. Because this cookie-type biscuit has no added fat, the result is a very hard and crunchy texture, perfect for dipping into dessert wine or hot coffee. Enjoy a variety of flavors. Biscotti freezes very well and stores well at room temperature in a covered container.

Choco-Choco Chip Biscotti

A great variation to the very popular almond biscotti. Makes 12 biscotti. Pictured on page 53.

All-purpose flour	**2 cups**	**500 mL**
Granulated sugar	**1 cup**	**250 mL**
Baking soda	**1 tsp.**	**5 mL**
Salt	**$1/_8$ tsp.**	**0.5 mL**
Cocoa	**$1/_2$ cup**	**125 mL**
Mini chocolate chips	**$1/_2$ cup**	**125 mL**
Large eggs	**2**	**2**
Egg whites (large)	**2**	**2**
Vanilla	**1 tsp.**	**5 mL**
Crème de Cacao or milk	**1 tbsp.**	**15 mL**

Combine first 6 ingredients in large bowl. ■ Combine eggs, egg whites, vanilla and Crème de Cacao in medium bowl. Beat with fork. Add to flour mixture. Mix. Dough will feel slightly dry. Lightly knead 8 to 10 times. Form into 16 inch (40 cm) oval roll that is $1^1/_2$ inches (3.8 cm) thick at the center. Place on lightly greased baking sheet. Bake in 350°F (175°C) oven for 30 minutes. Cool on wire rack for 10 minutes. Reduce heat to 325°F (160°C). Cut, slightly on the diagonal, into $1/_2$ inch (12 mm) slices. Bake, cut side down, on baking sheet for 10 to 12 minutes. Turn biscotti over and bake for 10 to 12 minutes, until crisp. Biscotti may be slightly soft in center but will harden when cooled. Remove to wire rack to cool.

Nutrition Information

1 biscotti: 216 Calories; 5 g Protein; 4.3 g Total Fat (2.2 g Sat., 36.2 mg Cholesterol);
166 mg Sodium

Apricot Raisin Biscotti

This biscotti is a little wider than the others because of the bulk of the fruit. Makes 12 biscotti. Pictured on page 53.

All-purpose flour	2$^1/_2$ **cups**	625 mL
Granulated sugar	**1 cup**	250 mL
Baking soda	**1 tsp.**	5 mL
Salt	$^1/_8$ **tsp.**	0.5 mL
Large eggs	**2**	2
Egg whites (large)	**2**	2
Almond flavoring	$^1/_2$ **tsp.**	2 mL
Finely chopped dried apricots	$^3/_4$ **cup**	175 mL
Chopped raisins	$^3/_4$ **cup**	175 mL
Prepared orange juice	**4 tsp.**	20 mL

Combine flour, sugar, baking soda and salt in large bowl. ■ Combine next 6 ingredients in medium bowl. Beat with fork. Add to dry mixture. Mix. Dough will feel slightly dry. Lightly knead 8 to 10 times. Form into 16 inch (40 cm) oval roll that is 1$^1/_2$ inches (3.5 cm) thick at the center. Place on lightly greased baking sheet. Bake in 350°F (175°C) oven for 30 minutes. Cool on wire rack for 10 minutes. Cut, slightly on the diagonal, into $^1/_2$ inch (12 mm) slices. Reduce heat to 325°F (160°C). Bake, cut side down, on baking sheet for 10 to 12 minutes. Turn biscotti over and bake for 10 to 12 minutes, until golden. Biscotti may be slightly soft in center but will harden when cooled. Remove to wire rack to cool.

Nutrition Information

1 biscotti: 223 Calories; 5 g Protein; 1.2 g Total Fat (0.3 g Sat., 35.9 mg Cholesterol); 165 mg Sodium

Almond Biscotti

To toast almonds, place in a microwave safe dish. Microwave, uncovered, on high (100%) power for 1$^1/_2$ to 2 minutes, stirring occasionally. Makes 12 biscotti. Pictured on page 53.

All-purpose flour	2$^1/_2$ **cups**	625 mL
Granulated sugar	**1 cup**	250 mL
Baking soda	**1 tsp.**	5 mL
Salt	$^1/_8$ **tsp.**	0.5 mL
Toasted chopped almonds	$^1/_2$ **cup**	125 mL
Large eggs	**2**	2
Egg whites (large)	**2**	2
Vanilla	$^1/_2$ **tsp.**	2 mL
Almond flavoring	$^1/_2$ **tsp.**	2 mL
Amaretto liqueur	**1$^1/_2$ tbsp.**	25 mL

(continued on next page)

Combine flour, sugar, baking soda, salt and almonds in large bowl. ■ Combine next 5 ingredients in medium bowl. Beat with fork. Add to dry mixture. Mix. Dough will feel slightly dry. Lightly knead 8 to 10 times. Form into 16 inch (40 cm) oval roll that is 1¹/₂ inches (3.8 cm) thick at the center. Place on lightly greased baking sheet. Bake in 350°F (175°C) oven for 30 minutes. Cool on wire rack for 10 minutes. Cut, slightly on the diagonal, into ¹/₂ inch (12 mm) slices. Reduce heat to 325°F (160°C). Bake, cut side down, on baking sheet for 10 to 12 minutes. Turn biscotti over and bake for 10 to 12 minutes, until golden. Biscotti may be slightly soft in center but will harden when cooled. Remove to wire rack to cool.

Nutrition Information

1 biscotti: 224 Calories; 6 g Protein; 4 g Total Fat (0.6 g Sat., 35.9 mg Cholesterol); 164 mg Sodium

Vanilla Nut Biscotti

Try using walnuts, hazelnuts, or your favorite kind of nut. Makes 12 biscotti. Pictured on page 53.

All-purpose flour	2¹/₂ cups	625 mL
Granulated sugar	1 cup	250 mL
Baking soda	1 tsp.	5 mL
Salt	¹/₈ tsp.	0.5 mL
Toasted chopped pecans	¹/₄ cup	60 mL
Large eggs	2	2
Egg whites (large)	2	2
Vanilla	2 tsp.	10 mL
Grated lemon peel	¹/₂ tsp.	2 mL
Freshly squeezed lemon juice	1 tsp.	5 mL
1% milk	1 tbsp.	15 mL

Combine flour, sugar, baking soda, salt and pecans in large bowl. ■ Combine next 6 ingredients in medium bowl. Beat with fork. Add to flour mixture. Mix. Dough will feel slightly dry. Turn out onto lightly floured surface. Gently knead dough 8 to 10 times. Form into 16 inch (40 cm) oval roll that is 1¹/₂ inches (3.8 cm) thick at the center. Place on lightly greased baking sheet. Bake in 350°F (175°C) oven for 30 minutes. Cool on wire rack for 10 minutes. Cut, slightly on the diagonal, into ¹/₂ inch (12 mm) slices. Reduce heat to 325°F (160°C). Bake, cut side down, on baking sheet for 10 to 12 minutes. Turn biscotti over and bake for 10 to 12 minutes until golden. Biscotti may be slightly soft in center but will harden when cooled. Remove to wire rack to cool.

Nutrition Information

1 biscotti: 203 Calories; 5 g Protein; 2.9 g Total Fat (0.5 g Sat., 36 mg Cholesterol); 164 mg Sodium

Angel Trifle

A great company dessert that can be made the night before. Serves 12. Pictured on page 54.

Custard powder	3 tbsp.	50 mL
Granulated sugar	1/4 cup	60 mL
Skim evaporated milk	13 1/2 oz.	385 mL
Skim milk	1 cup	250 mL
Almond flavoring	1 tsp.	5 mL
Strawberry-flavored gelatin (jelly powder)	1 × 3 oz.	1 × 85 g
Boiling water	1 cup	250 mL
Reserved mandarin orange liquid	1/2 cup	125 mL
Baked white angel food cake (commercial mix), torn into medium-size pieces	1	1
Fresh strawberries sliced	1 cup	250 mL
Canned mandarin orange segments, drained, liquid reserved	10 oz.	284 mL
Envelope dessert topping (such as Dream Whip)	1	1
Skim milk	1/2 cup	125 mL
Fresh strawberries, sliced	1 cup	250 mL

Combine custard and sugar in saucepan. Add evaporated milk and skim milk. Heat, whisking until boiling. Remove from heat. Let stand for 15 minutes. Stir in almond flavoring. Cover surface with plastic wrap. Refrigerate. ■ Combine gelatin, boiling water and mandarin orange liquid. Stir until gelatin is dissolved. Refrigerate until syrupy. ■ Place 1/3 cake pieces in large glass bowl. Sprinkle 1 cup (250 mL) strawberries over cake. Drizzle 1/2 custard over top. Pour 1/2 syrupy gelatin over custard. Place another 1/3 layer cake pieces on top of gelatin. Sprinkle with orange pieces. Drizzle remaining gelatin over oranges. Add remaining 1/3 cake pieces and remaining 1/2 custard. ■ Beat dessert topping and milk together according to package directions. Pipe over top of custard. Garnish with strawberries. Chill several hours or overnight.

Nutrition Information

1 serving: 275 Calories; 9 g Protein; 1.8 g Total Fat (1.4 g Sat., 1.8 mg Cholesterol); 178 mg Sodium

Apples In A Phyllo Crust

For a softer pastry, cool and cover with plastic wrap. Let stand for three hours or overnight. Serves 8 to 10. Pictured on page 54.

Cooking apples (such as McIntosh),peeled, cored and sliced into thin wedges	6	6
Lemon juice, fresh or bottled	2 tbsp.	30 mL
Brown sugar, packed	1 cup	250 mL
Minute tapioca	2 tbsp.	30 mL
Ground cinnamon	1/2 tsp.	2 mL
Phyllo pastry sheets	3	3
Canola oil (or use cooking spray)	2 tsp.	10 mL
Graham cracker crumbs	1/4 cup	60 mL
Granulated sugar	2 tsp.	10 mL
Ground cinnamon	1/4 tsp.	1 mL

Place apple wedges in large saucepan. Add lemon juice, brown sugar, tapioca and cinnamon. Stir. Let stand for 10 minutes. Heat on low, stirring constantly, until sugar is dissolved and apples are partially cooked. Cool. ■ Lightly oil 1 side of each phyllo sheet. Sprinkle with light dusting of graham crumbs. 1. Center pastry sheets, crumb-side up, spiral-fashion, in ungreased 10 inch (25 cm) glass pie plate, letting some pastry hang over edge. 2. Pour apple filling over pastry sheets. 3. Fold overhanging pastry sheets over filling. Lightly oil surface of folded pastry. ■ Sprinkle with sugar and cinnamon. Bake on bottom rack in 350°F (175°C) oven for 30 minutes until golden. Cool.

N u t r i t i o n   I n f o r m a t i o n

1/8 recipe: 204 Calories; 1 g Protein; 1.6 g Total Fat (0.4 g Sat., 0 mg Cholesterol); 50 mg Sodium

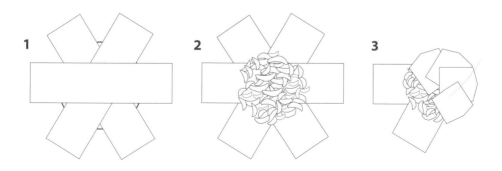

Pumpkin Mousse

Serve this in dessert bowls or in a Graham Crust, page 32. Makes 4¹/₂ cups (1.1 L).

Envelopes unflavored gelatin	**2 × ¹/₄ oz.**	**2 × 7 g**
Cold water	**¹/₂ cup**	**125 mL**
Brown sugar, packed	**¹/₂ cup**	**125 mL**
Canned pumpkin	**14 oz.**	**398 mL**
Vanilla	**1 tsp.**	**5 mL**
Ground cinnamon	**¹/₄ tsp.**	**1 mL**
Ground nutmeg	**¹/₈ tsp.**	**0.5 mL**
Ground ginger	**¹/₂ tsp.**	**2 mL**
Salt, sprinkle		
Envelope dessert topping (such as Dream Whip)	**1**	**1**
Skim milk	**¹/₂ cup**	**125 mL**

Sprinkle gelatin over water in medium saucepan. Stir. Let stand for 1 minute. Heat gently, adding brown sugar. Stir until gelatin and sugar are dissolved. ■ Add next 6 ingredients. Stir together well. Remove from heat. Chill, stirring occasionally, for 45 to 60 minutes until thickened. ■ Beat dessert topping and skim milk together according to package directions. Beat pumpkin mixture until light and fluffy. Fold dessert topping into pumpkin mixture. Chill until set.

Nutrition Information

¹/₂ cup (125 mL): 57 Calories; 3 g Protein; 2 g Total Fat (1.8 g Sat., 0.3 mg Cholesterol); 17 mg Sodium

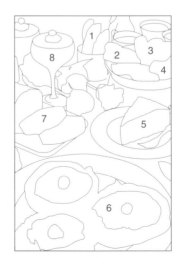

1. Apricot Raisin Biscotti, page 48
2. Almond Biscotti, page 48
3. Choco-Choco Chip Biscotti, page 47
4. Vanilla Nut Biscotti, page 49
5. French Chocolate Dessert, page 64
6. Chocolate On A Cloud, page 59
7. Latté Cake Roll, page 45
8. Chocolate Mousse Parfaits, page 56

Creamy Pudding

Garnish with fresh fruit in between pudding layers in a dessert bowl or pour pudding into a prepared pie shell and garnish the top with fresh fruit. The pudding sets quickly. Makes 5¹/₂ cups (1.3 L).

Pineapple juice	**1 cup**	**250 mL**
Envelope unflavored gelatin	**1 × ¹/₄ oz.**	**1 × 7 g**
Lemon-flavored gelatin (jelly powder)	**1 × 3 oz.**	**1 × 85 g**
Light cream cheese, cut into 8 squares	**8 oz.**	**250 g**
Non-fat cottage cheese	**1 cup**	**250 mL**
Low-fat frozen whipped topping (such as Light Cool Whip), thawed	**4 cups**	**1 L**

Pour pineapple juice into small saucepan. Sprinkle with unflavored gelatin. Let stand for 5 minutes. Heat and stir until gelatin is dissolved. Remove from heat. Stir in lemon-flavored gelatin. Stir until dissolved. ■ Put cream cheese and cottage cheese in blender or food processor. Process, gradually adding hot gelatin mixture, until smooth. Drop spoonfuls of whipped topping into blender. Pulse until blended.

N u t r i t i o n   I n f o r m a t i o n

¹/₂ cup (125 mL): 179 Calories; 8 g Protein; 7.6 g Total Fat (5.8 g Sat., 11.4 mg Cholesterol); 287 mg Sodium

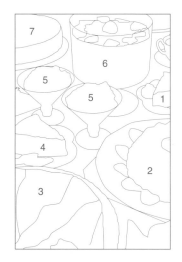

1. No-Guilt Cheese Torte, page 62
2. Fresh Is Best Mousse, page 60
3. Apples In A Phyllo Crust, page 51
4. Cherry Fluff Dessert, page 61
5. Peach Chiffon Dessert, page 58
6. Angel Trifle, page 50
7. Lemon Fluff Dessert, page 61

Mocha Sorbetto

Sorbetto is the Italian word for sherbet. After the initial 45 minutes freezing time, the espresso mixture can be completed in an ice cream maker. Makes 8 cups (2 L).

Hot espresso coffee (or use double strength regular coffee)	3¹/₂ cups	875 mL
Granulated sugar	²/₃ cup	150 mL
Cocoa	2 tbsp.	30 mL
Skim evaporated milk	13¹/₂ oz.	385 mL

Chill 9 x 13 inch (22 x 33 cm) pan in freezer. Pour hot coffee into medium bowl. ■ Combine sugar and cocoa in small bowl. Add to hot coffee. Beat together until dissolved. ■ Stir in evaporated milk. Pour into cold pan. Freeze for 45 minutes. Stir, bringing any crystals to center. Freeze for about 2 hours until hard. Use fork to break into chunks. Process in food processor until smooth. Freeze until serving time.

N u t r i t i o n   I n f o r m a t i o n

¹/₂ cup (125 mL): 58 Calories; 2 g Protein; 0.1 g Total Fat (trace Sat., 0.9 mg Cholesterol); 33 mg Sodium

Chocolate Mousse Parfaits

Mousse is a French term meaning "froth" or "foam". The fluffiness is due to the addition of dessert topping. Makes 6 parfaits. Pictured on page 53.

Envelope unflavored gelatin	1 x ¹/₄ oz.	1 x 7 g
Granulated sugar	¹/₂ cup	125 mL
Cocoa	¹/₃ cup	75 mL
Salt, sprinkle		
Egg yolks (large), fork-beaten	2	2
Skim evaporated milk	13¹/₂ oz.	385 mL
Skim milk	²/₃ cup	150 mL
Vanilla	2 tsp.	10 mL
Egg whites (large)	2	2
Envelope dessert topping (such as Dream Whip), divided	1	1
Skim milk	¹/₂ cup	125 mL
Chocolate wafer crumbs	³/₄ cup	175 mL
Chocolate covered coffee beans (optional)	6	6

(continued on next page)

Combine gelatin, sugar, cocoa and salt in medium saucepan. Add egg yolks and evaporated milk. Whisk together. Let stand for 2 minutes. Heat mixture on medium-low for 10 minutes, whisking constantly until smooth and slightly thickened. ■ Stir in first amount of skim milk and vanilla. Remove from heat. Cool, stirring several times, until mixture is slightly gelled and able to mound. ■ Beat egg whites together until soft peaks form. Gradually add gelatin mixture, beating constantly until fluffy and doubled in volume. ■ Beat dessert topping and second amount of skim milk together according to package directions. Fold 1 cup (250 mL) into egg white mixture. Fill 6 parfait glasses each with ¹/₃ cup (75 mL) mousse. Sprinkle 1 tbsp. (15 mL) wafer crumbs on top. Repeat. Top each with remaining mousse. ■ Pipe remaining 1 cup (250 mL) dessert topping over mousse layer. Top each parfait with coffee bean. Chill at least 1¹/₂ hours before serving.

Nutrition Information

1 parfait: 274 Calories; 11 g Protein; 7.4 g Total Fat (4.1 g Sat., 78.3 mg Cholesterol); 136 mg Sodium

Whipped Topping

Make this up to one hour ahead of time. Makes 4 cups (1 L). Pictured on page 35.

Skim milk powder	¹/₂ **cup**	**125 mL**
Water	1¹/₃ **cup**	**325 mL**
Envelope unflavored gelatin	1 × ¹/₄ **oz.**	**1 × 7 g**
Cold water	**3 tbsp.**	**50 mL**
Granulated sugar	¹/₃ **cup**	**75 mL**
Vanilla	1¹/₂ **tsp.**	**7 mL**

Combine milk powder and water in saucepan and heat until milk is very hot but not boiling. Remove from heat. ■ Combine gelatin and water in small bowl. Let stand for 1 minute to soften gelatin. ■ Add gelatin mixture and sugar to hot milk. Stir until dissolved. Chill in refrigerator until milk mixture is cold and slightly thickened. Beat on high for about 8 minutes or until consistency of soft whipped cream. Beat in vanilla. Keep at room temperature. Do not chill or it will gel.

Nutrition Information

2 tbsp. (30 mL): 16 Calories; 1 g Protein; trace Total Fat (trace Sat., 0.4 mg Cholesterol); 10 mg Sodium

Peach Chiffon Dessert

This looks lovely garnished with Whipped Topping, page 57, and sliced peaches. Perfect after any meal. Try this poured into a cooked Corn Flake Crust, page31, then chilled. Serves 10. Pictured on page 54.

Envelopes unflavored gelatin	**2 × $^1/_4$ oz.**	**2 × 7 g**
Cold water	**$^1/_2$ cup**	**125 mL**
Reserved peach juice		
Strained peaches (baby food)	**2 × 4$^1/_2$ oz.**	**2 × 128 g**
Granulated sugar	**$^2/_3$ cup**	**150 mL**
Lemon juice, fresh or bottled	**2 tsp.**	**10 mL**
Egg whites (large)	**2**	**2**
Low-fat frozen whipped topping, (such as Light Cool Whip), thawed	**1 cup**	**250 mL**
Sliced peaches, drained, juice reserved	**14 oz.**	**398 mL**

Combine gelatin with water in small saucepan. Let stand for 1 minute. Add reserved peach juice, strained peaches, sugar and lemon juice. Stir. Heat on low, stirring constantly, until gelatin and sugar are dissolved. Chill until slightly thickened. ■ Beat egg whites together in small bowl until foamy. Add peach mixture. Beat on high, about 10 minutes, until light and fluffy. Beat in whipped topping. Fold in peaches. Pour into large bowl or individual serving dishes. Chill until firm.

Nutrition Information

1 serving: 111 Calories; 2 g Protein; 1.1 g Total Fat (1 g Sat., 0 mg Cholesterol); 20 mg Sodium

Lemon Sherbet

Serve small scoops for a light cool dessert. Double the recipe if you are serving more. Makes 2$^1/_2$ cups (625 mL).

Yogurt Cheese, page 67	**1$^1/_2$ cups**	**375 mL**
Granulated sugar	**1 cup**	**250 mL**
Juice and grated peel of 1 lemon		
Frozen whipped topping (such as Cool Whip), thawed	**$^1/_2$ cup**	**125 mL**

Beat yogurt cheese, sugar, lemon juice and lemon peel together on low until smooth. ■ Fold whipped topping into yogurt cheese mixture. Pour into 8 × 8 inch (20 × 20 cm) pan. Freeze for 8 hours or overnight until firm.

Nutrition Information

$^1/_2$ cup (125 mL): 270 Calories; 8 g Protein; 2.2 g Total Fat (1.8 g Sat., 2.9 mg Cholesterol); 114 mg Sodium

Chocolate On A Cloud

Perfect to serve for a small dinner party. Double the recipe for a larger crowd. Makes 4 filled meringues. Pictured on page 53.

MERINGUE		
Egg whites (large)	**3**	**3**
Cream of tartar	**$^1/_4$ tsp.**	**1 mL**
Salt, sprinkle		
Vanilla	**$^1/_2$ tsp.**	**2 mL**
Granulated sugar	**$^1/_2$ cup**	**125 mL**
TIA MARIA FILLING		
Cornstarch	**3 tbsp.**	**50 mL**
All-purpose flour	**3 tbsp.**	**50 mL**
Granulated sugar	**$^1/_3$ cup**	**75 mL**
Cocoa	**$^1/_4$ cup**	**60 mL**
Salt, sprinkle		
Skim evaporated milk	**1$^2/_3$ cups**	**400 mL**
Vanilla	**1 tsp.**	**5 mL**
Tia Maria liqueur	**$^1/_4$ cup**	**60 mL**

Chocolate curls, for garnish

Meringue: Draw four, 4 inch (10 cm) circles on brown paper or parchment paper on baking sheet. Beat egg whites, cream of tartar and salt together in medium bowl. Beat in vanilla. Gradually beat in sugar until stiff peaks form. Pipe meringue onto paper circles, covering bottom and building up sides to make shell. Another method is to spoon meringue onto paper circles, forming a shell with back of spoon. (Shell should be deep enough to hold about $^1/_2$ cup, 125 mL, filling). Bake in 300°F (150°C) oven for 30 minutes. Turn oven off. Leave meringues in oven for 1 hour to dry. Remove. Cool to room temperature. ■ **Tia Maria Filling:** Combine cornstarch, flour, sugar, cocoa and salt in medium saucepan. Whisk in evaporated milk. Heat, stirring frequently, until thickened. Remove from heat. Whisk in vanilla and Tia Maria. Place plastic wrap directly onto filling surface. Cool. Makes 2 cups (500 mL) filling. ■ Spoon filling into cooled meringues. Garnish with chocolate curls.

Nutrition Information

1 meringue with $^1/_2$ cup (125 mL) filling: 388 Calories; 13 g Protein; 0.8 g Total Fat (0.4 g Sat., 4.1 mg Cholesterol); 196 mg Sodium; good source of Fiber

Fresh Is Best Mousse

Garnish this mousse with sliced fresh fruit. Serve this as a dessert or as an accompaniment with pork or veal. Serves 8. Pictured on page 54.

Envelopes unflavored gelatin	2 × $^1/_4$ oz.	2 × 7 g
Freshly squeezed or prepared orange juice	1 cup	250 mL
Granulated sugar	$^1/_2$ cup	125 mL
Lemon juice, fresh or bottled	$^1/_4$ cup	60 mL
Grated lemon peel	$^1/_2$ tsp.	2 mL
Grated orange peel	$^1/_2$ tsp.	2 mL
Banana, mashed	1	1
Mashed fresh strawberries	1 cup	250 mL
Envelope dessert topping (such as Dream Whip)	1	1
Skim milk	$^1/_2$ cup	125 mL
Egg whites (large)	3	3

Combine gelatin and $^1/_2$ cup (125 mL) orange juice in small saucepan. Let stand 1 minute. Add remaining $^1/_2$ cup (125 mL) orange juice and sugar. Heat and stir until sugar and gelatin are dissolved. Remove from heat. ■ Stir in lemon juice, lemon peel and orange peel. Pour mixture into large bowl. Cool slightly. ■ Add banana and strawberries. Refrigerate until mixture is slightly thickened. ■ Beat dessert topping and skim milk together according to package directions. Fold into orange juice mixture. ■ Whip egg whites until soft peaks form. Fold into orange juice mixture. Spoon into large decorative bowl or ring mold or into soufflé dish with waxed paper collar. Chill until firm.

N u t r i t i o n   I n f o r m a t i o n

1 serving: 136 Calories; 4 g Protein; 2.4 g Total Fat (2 g Sat., 0.3 mg Cholesterol); 38 mg Sodium

· ·

Use whipped topping (powdered or frozen) instead of whipped cream. Frozen topping will reduce fat grams by 50%; powdered topping, whipped with skim milk, will reduce fat grams by about 80%.

Lemon Fluff Dessert

Use any flavor of gelatin for this dessert. Cuts into 10 pieces. Pictured on page 54 and on the front cover.

Graham wafer crumbs	1¹/₂ **cups**	**375 mL**
Diet tub margarine, melted	¹/₃ **cup**	**75 mL**
Lemon-flavored gelatin (jelly powder)	**2 × 3 oz.**	**2 × 85 g**
Boiling water	1¹/₂ **cups**	**375 mL**
Yogurt Cheese, page 67	**1 cup**	**250 mL**
Granulated sugar	**1 cup**	**250 mL**
Skim evaporated milk (chilled in freezer until icy cold)	13¹/₂ **oz.**	**385 mL**
Lemon juice, fresh or bottled	**3 tbsp.**	**50 mL**

Combine crumbs and melted margarine in bowl. Reserve ¹/₄ cup (60 mL) for topping. Pack evenly and firmly into 10 inch (25 cm) springform pan. Bake in 350°F (175°C) oven for 10 minutes. Cool. ■ Stir gelatin and boiling water together until dissolved. Chill until syrupy, stirring occasionally to keep smooth. ■ Beat yogurt cheese and sugar together until smooth. Refrigerate. ■ Beat evaporated milk with lemon juice in large bowl on high until stiff. Add slightly thickened gelatin mixture. Beat until light and fluffy. Fold in yogurt mixture. Pour over graham crust. Sprinkle with reserved crumbs. Chill until set.

Nutrition Information

1 piece: 298 Calories; 9 g Protein; 4.9 g Total Fat (1.1 g Sat., 2.5 mg Cholesterol); 326 mg Sodium

CHERRY FLUFF DESSERT: Substitute cherry-flavored gelatin (jelly powder) for lemon. Pictured on page 54.

Have fresh fruit at the end of a meal instead of high-fat dessert.

No-Guilt Cheese Torte

For a raspberry sauce, use frozen raspberries in place of strawberries. Serves 12. Pictured on page 54.

Graham cracker crumbs	2¹/₄ cups	560 mL
Granulated sugar	2 tbsp.	30 mL
Egg whites (large)	2	2
Ground cinnamon	2 tsp.	10 mL
Envelopes unflavored gelatin	2 × ¹/₄ oz.	2 × 7 g
Cold water	¹/₂ cup	125 mL
Egg yolks (large)	2	2
Granulated sugar	¹/₂ cup	125 mL
Skim evaporated milk	¹/₂ cup	125 mL
Salt	¹/₂ tsp.	2 mL
Dry curd cottage cheese	2 cups	500 mL
Juice and grated peel of 1 lemon		
Egg whites (large)	2	2
Envelope dessert topping (such as Dream Whip)	1	1
Skim milk	¹/₃ cup	75 mL
STRAWBERRY SAUCE		
Reserved strawberry syrup		
Cornstarch	1 tbsp.	15 mL
Frozen strawberries with syrup, drained, syrup reserved	15 oz.	425 g

Combine graham crumbs, first amount of sugar, first amount of egg whites and cinnamon in blender. Process until graham crumbs are moistened. Reserve ¹/₄ cup (60 mL) for topping. Press remaining crumbs firmly in bottom and 1 inch (2.5 cm) up sides of 9 inch (22 cm) springform pan. Bake in 325°F (160°C) oven for 15 minutes. Cool. ■ Combine gelatin and water in small bowl. Stir. Let stand for 1 minute until gelatin is soft. ■ Combine next 4 ingredients in double boiler over boiling water. Whisk until thick like soft custard. Whisk in softened gelatin until dissolved. ■ Push cottage cheese through sieve to break up lumps. Add cottage cheese, lemon juice and lemon peel to milk mixture. Refrigerate until slightly thickened. ■ Beat second amount egg whites together in medium bowl until stiff peaks form. Beat dessert topping and milk together in separate bowl until stiff. Fold egg whites and dessert topping into thickened cottage cheese mixture. Pour over crust. Sprinkle with reserved graham crumbs. Chill for several hours or overnight until set. ■ **Strawberry Sauce:** Heat reserved syrup and cornstarch together in small saucepan until boiling and thickened. Cool slightly. Stir in strawberries. Drizzle over wedges of torte.

Nutrition Information

1 serving: 230 Calories; 10 g Protein; 4.5 g Total Fat (2.1 g Sat., 38.2 mg Cholesterol); 303 mg Sodium

Tiramisu

A low-fat version of the original! Store this in the freezer and take out as needed. Cuts into 12 pieces. Pictured on the front cover.

Non-fat spreadable cream cheese	**8 oz.**	**225 g**
Yogurt Cheese, page 67	**$^1/_2$ cup**	**125 mL**
Icing (confectioner's) sugar, sifted	**$^3/_4$ cup**	**175 mL**
Envelope dessert topping (such as Dream Whip)	**1**	**1**
Skim milk	**$^1/_2$ cup**	**125 mL**
Granulated sugar	**$^1/_3$ cup**	**75 mL**
Water	**3 tbsp.**	**50 mL**
Egg whites (large)	**2**	**2**
Ladyfingers, approximately	**40**	**40**
Hot double strength prepared coffee	**$^3/_4$ cup**	**175 mL**
Granulated sugar	**1 tbsp.**	**15 mL**
Kahlua liqueur	**3 tbsp.**	**50 mL**
Cocoa	**1-2 tsp.**	**5-10 mL**

Beat cream cheese, yogurt cheese and icing sugar together in large bowl until smooth. ■ Beat dessert topping and skim milk together according to package directions. Fold $^1/_2$ dessert topping into cheese mixture. ■ Combine granulated sugar, water and egg whites in top of double boiler over simmering water. Beat on high, over simmering water, until stiff peaks form. Gently fold egg white mixture into cheese mixture. Set aside. ■ Lay $^1/_2$ ladyfingers in single layer in bottom of foil-lined 9 × 9 inch (22 × 22 cm) pan. ■ Combine coffee with sugar and Kahlua. Drizzle $^1/_2$ coffee mixture over ladyfingers. Spread with $^1/_2$ cheese mixture. Repeat with another layer of ladyfingers, coffee mixture and cheese mixture. Top with thin layer remaining $^1/_2$ dessert topping. ■ Lightly sprinkle with cocoa. Freeze for about 2 hours.

Nutrition Information

1 piece: 204 Calories; 5 g Protein; 3.2 g Total Fat (2.1 g Sat., 2.8 mg Cholesterol); 51 mg Sodium

Use skim or 1% milk instead of 2% or whole milk. One cup (250 mL) skim milk contains 0.5 grams of fat; 1% contains 2.7 grams of fat; 2% contains 5 grams of fat; homogenized (whole) milk contains 8.6 grams of fat.

French Chocolate Dessert

Toasted almonds may be used on top as a garnish instead of being used inside the dessert. Cuts into 12 pieces. Pictured on page 53.

Envelopes unflavored gelatin	2 × 1/4 oz.	2 × 7 g
Granulated sugar	1/2 **cup**	125 mL
Cocoa	1/2 **cup**	125 mL
Egg yolks (large)	2	2
Skim evaporated milk	13 1/2 oz.	385 mL
Skim milk	1 cup	250 mL
Amaretto liqueur	1/2 **cup**	125 mL
Egg whites (large)	2	2
Envelope dessert topping (such as Dream Whip)	1	1
Skim milk	1/2 **cup**	125 mL
Vanilla	1 tsp.	5 mL
Chocolate wafer crumbs	1/2 **cup**	125 mL
Chocolate Angel Food Cake, page 29 or 34, cut into bite-size pieces (about 1/2 cake)	4 cups	1 L
Toasted slivered almonds	2 tbsp.	30 mL
Chocolate chips, melted (optional)	1/4 **cup**	60 mL

Combine gelatin, sugar and cocoa in medium saucepan. Beat egg yolks and evaporated milk together in small bowl. Add to cocoa mixture. Heat on medium-low, whisking constantly, until gelatin is dissolved and slightly thickened. ■ Whisk in first amount of skim milk and liqueur. Refrigerate, stirring occasionally, until thickened. ■ Beat egg whites until soft peaks form. Gradually add gelatin mixture, beating until fluffy. ■ Beat dessert topping, second amount of skim milk and vanilla together according to package directions. Beat into gelatin mixture. ■ Lightly grease sides and bottom of 10 inch (25 cm) springform pan. Sprinkle sides and bottom of pan with wafer crumbs. Place 2 cups (250 mL) cake pieces on top of crumbs in single layer. Pour 1/2 chocolate mixture evenly over cake pieces. Shake pan to fill in any spaces. Sprinkle with toasted almonds. Layer remaining cake pieces over almonds. Pour remaining chocolate mixture over cake. Smooth evenly. ■ Drizzle with melted chocolate if desired. Chill several hours.

Nutrition Information

1 piece: 234 Calories; 9 g Protein; 4.2 g Total Fat (2.1 g Sat., 39 mg Cholesterol); 108 mg Sodium

Gingerbread With Marshmallow Cheese

Lightly grease the measuring cup before measuring marshmallow cream. It will slide out nicely. Cuts into 15 pieces.

All-purpose flour	1$^1/_2$ cups	375 mL
Whole wheat flour	$^3/_4$ cup	175 mL
Brown sugar, packed	$^1/_2$ cup	125 mL
Ground ginger	1 tbsp.	15 mL
Ground cinnamon	1 tsp.	5 mL
Baking powder	$^1/_2$ tsp.	2 mL
Baking soda	2 tsp.	10 mL
Egg whites (large), fork-beaten	3	3
1% buttermilk	$^3/_4$ cup	175 mL
Applesauce	$^1/_2$ cup	125 mL
Hard margarine, melted	$^1/_4$ cup	60 mL
Mild molasses	$^1/_2$ cup	125 mL
MARSHMALLOW CHEESE		
Light spreadable cream cheese	4 oz.	125 g
Marshmallow cream	$^1/_2$ cup	125 mL
Vanilla	1 tsp.	5 mL
Lemon juice, fresh or bottled	$^1/_2$ tsp.	2 mL
Icing (confectioner's) sugar	$^3/_4$ cup	175 mL

Combine first 7 ingredients in large bowl. ■ Combine next 5 ingredients in small bowl. Beat buttermilk mixture into flour mixture until smooth. Pour batter into lightly greased 9 × 13 inch (22 × 33 cm) pan. Spread evenly. Bake in 350°F (175°C) oven for 30 minutes until wooden pick inserted in center comes out clean. ■ **Marshmallow Cheese:** Beat all 5 ingredients together in bowl until smooth. Top each piece with 1 tbsp. (15 mL) Marshmallow Cheese.

Nutrition Information

1 piece: 211 Calories; 4 g Protein; 4.8 g Total Fat (1.5 g Sat., 4.6 mg Cholesterol); 338 mg Sodium

Use non-fat frozen yogurt, sherbet or ice milk instead of ice cream.

Dips & Spreads

When we think about dips and spreads we often think about added fat we probably don't need. Not anymore! Sample this variety of delicious dips for fruit and vegetables. These spreads are great on bagels, bread slices or crackers.

Maple Nut Cheese

Spread on graham crackers or wedges of apple and pear. Makes 1 cup (250 mL).

Vanilla Yogurt Cheese, page 67	1 cup	250 mL
Maple flavoring	1/8 tsp.	0.5 mL
Dark corn syrup	1 1/2 tbsp.	25 mL
Finely chopped walnuts	1 tbsp.	15 mL

Combine yogurt cheese, maple flavoring and corn syrup in small bowl. Beat until smooth. ■ Add walnuts. Stir together.

Nutrition Information

2 tbsp. (30 mL): 50 Calories; 3 g Protein; 0.7 g Total Fat (0.1 g Sat., 1.2 mg Cholesterol); 47 mg Sodium

Honey Mustard Dip

A hint of tartness to this dip. Store in the refrigerator for up to one week. Makes 1 cup (250 mL).

Liquid honey	6 tbsp.	100 mL
Apple juice	2 tbsp.	30 mL
Prepared mustard	2 tbsp.	30 mL
Low-fat salad dressing (or mayonnaise)	1/3 cup	75 mL
Non-fat sour cream	1/3 cup	75 mL

Combine all 5 ingredients in small bowl. Whisk until smooth.

Nutrition Information

2 tbsp. (30 mL): 93 Calories; 1 g Protein; 2.7 g Total Fat (0.1 g Sat., 0 mg Cholesterol); 130 mg Sodium

Yogurt Cheese

A wonderful substitute for cream cheese or sour cream. Store in a covered container in the refrigerator until the expiry date of the yogurt. Makes 2 cups (500 mL).

Plain skim milk yogurt (without gelatin)	**4 cups**	**1 L**

Line strainer with 2 layers of cheesecloth and place over deep bowl. Spoon yogurt into strainer. Cover loosely with plastic wrap. Drain for 24 hours in refrigerator. Discard whey in bowl several times as yogurt drains. Store yogurt cheese in covered container in refrigerator.

Nutrition Information

$^1/_2$ cup (125 mL): 131 Calories; 13 g Protein; 0.3 g Total Fat (0.2 g Sat., 4.8 mg Cholesterol); 185 mg Sodium

VANILLA YOGURT CHEESE: Use vanilla-flavored skim milk yogurt (without gelatin) instead of plain skim milk yogurt.

Honey Yogurt Fruit Dip

Keep chilled until ready to serve with fruit or graham crackers. Makes 2 cups (500 mL).

Yogurt Cheese, above	**1 cup**	**250 mL**
Liquid honey	**$^1/_4$ cup**	**60 mL**
Low-fat frozen whipped topping (such as Light Cool Whip), thawed	**1 cup**	**250 mL**

Combine yogurt cheese, liquid honey and whipped topping in blender. Process until smooth. Chill.

Nutrition Information

2 tbsp. (30 mL): 47 Calories; 2 g Protein; 1.2 g Total Fat (1.1 g Sat., 0.6 mg Cholesterol); 24 mg Sodium

Variation: Add either $^1/_4$ tsp. (1 mL) ground cinnamon, 1 tsp. (5 mL) grated lemon peel or 1 tsp. (5 mL) vanilla.

Try yogurt cheese, above, flavored with garlic and herbs, as a sandwich spread.

tip

Easy Onion Dip

Great for baked potato chips or vegetables. Makes 1¹/₄ cups (300 mL).

1% creamed cottage cheese	**1 cup**	**250 mL**
1% buttermilk	**¹/₄ cup**	**60 mL**
Garlic powder	**¹/₈ tsp.**	**0.5 mL**
Beef bouillon powder	**1 tsp.**	**5 mL**
Minced onion flakes	**1 tbsp.**	**15 mL**

Combine all 5 ingredients in blender. Process until fairly smooth. Refrigerate for several hours or overnight until onion is soft.

Nutrition Information

2 tbsp. (30 mL): 25 Calories; 4 g Protein; 0.4 g Total Fat (0.2 g Sat., 1.4 mg Cholesterol); 175 mg Sodium

Fruit Spread

Delicious on toasted bagels. Store in the refrigerator for two or three days. Makes 1¹/₂ cups (375 mL). Pictured on page 89.

Dried apricots, coarsely chopped	**15**	**15**
Prepared orange juice	**1 cup**	**250 mL**
Vanilla Yogurt Cheese, page 67	**¹/₂ cup**	**125 mL**
Non-fat spreadable cream cheese	**¹/₂ cup**	**125 mL**
Brown sugar, packed	**2 tsp.**	**10 mL**
Ground cinnamon (optional)	**¹/₈ tsp.**	**0.5 mL**
Ground cardamom (optional)	**¹/₈ tsp.**	**0.5 mL**

Combine apricots and orange juice in small saucepan. Bring to a boil. Reduce heat. Simmer for 15 minutes until apricots are soft, stirring often. Remove from heat. Cover and cool. ■ Combine apricot mixture with remaining 5 ingredients in blender. Process until smooth. Chill.

Nutrition Information

2 tbsp. (30 mL): 41 Calories; 2 g Protein; 0.1 g Total Fat (0.3 g Sat., 2 mg Cholesterol); 111 mg Sodium

Use fruit spreads, jams or jellies instead of butter or margarine in sandwiches, on crackers or on toast.

Greek Cucumber Spread

Use a plastic colander to drain the cucumber. Metal colanders will alter taste of the cucumber.
Serve on pita bread wedges. Makes about 3 cups (750 mL). Pictured on page 17.

English cucumber, with peel, grated	1	1
Salt	1¹/₂ **tsp.**	7 mL
Yogurt Cheese, page 67	**2 cups**	500 mL
Garlic cloves, crushed	2-3	2-3
Lemon pepper	¹/₂ **tsp.**	2 mL

Combine cucumber and salt in large plastic colander in sink or over bowl. Let stand at room temperature for 1 hour. Push down on cucumber, draining out as much liquid as possible. Place in medium bowl. ■ Add yogurt cheese, garlic and lemon pepper. Refrigerate for at least 1 hour to allow flavors to blend.

Nutrition Information

2 tbsp. (30 mL): 23 Calories; 2 g Protein; 0.1 g Total Fat; (trace Sat., 0.8 mg Cholesterol); 193 mg Sodium

Bean And Corn Salsa

Serve with tortilla chips, or as a condiment with chicken or beef dishes Try heating and serving over pasta. Store in the refrigerator in a covered container for up to one week. Makes 5 cups (1.25 L).
Pictured on page 17.

Chunky salsa, mild or medium	1¹/₃ **cups**	325 mL
Canned kernel corn, drained	**12 oz.**	341 mL
Canned black beans, drained (or 1 cup,	**14 oz.**	398 mL
250 mL, cooked)		
Medium red onion, finely diced	¹/₂	¹/₂
Finely diced green or red pepper	¹/₂ **cup**	125 mL
Chili powder	¹/₂ **tsp.**	2 mL
Cayenne pepper, sprinkle		
Finely chopped fresh cilantro	**2 tbsp.**	30 mL

Combine all 8 ingredients in medium bowl. Let stand for about 30 minutes to blend flavors.

Nutrition Information

¹/₄ cup (60 mL): 40 Calories; 2 g Protein; 0.3 g Total Fat (0.1 g Sat., 0 mg Cholesterol); 136 mg Sodium

Smoked Salmon Spread

Serve on stoned wheat crackers or melba toast. Pack into a serving bowl and garnish with fresh parsley. Makes 2¹/₂ cups (625 mL).

Low-fat ricotta cheese	**2 cups**	**500 mL**
Skim milk yogurt	**1 cup**	**250 mL**
Canned red sockeye salmon, well drained, skin and bones removed	**7¹/₂ oz.**	**213 g**
Garlic clove, crushed	**1**	**1**
Hickory smoke flavoring	**¹/₈ tsp.**	**0.5 mL**
Prepared horseradish	**1 tsp.**	**5 mL**
Lemon juice, fresh or bottled	**1 tsp.**	**5 mL**
Finely chopped green onion	**2 tbsp.**	**30 mL**
Salt	**¹/₂ tsp.**	**2 mL**
Pepper	**¹/₈ tsp.**	**0.5 mL**

Combine cheese and yogurt in blender. Process until smooth. Line a sieve with 2 layers of cheesecloth. Place over deep bowl. Pour in cheese mixture. Cover with plastic wrap. Drain for 24 hours. ■ Put drained cheese into medium bowl. Add remaining 8 ingredients. Mix well.

Nutrition Information

2 tbsp. (30 mL): 58 Calories; 5 g Protein; 3 g Total Fat (1.5 g Sat., 10.5 mg Cholesterol); 148 mg Sodium

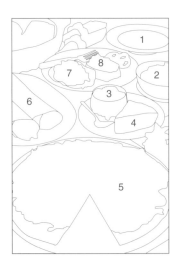

1. Garlic And Onion Soup, page 137
2. Curried Shrimp With Couscous, page 85
3. Three Tomato Sauce, page 132
4. Polenta Wedges, page 78
5. Roasted Vegetable Focaccia, page 83
6. Chicken Fajitas, page 77
7. Mediterranean Salad, page 130
8. Shrimp Frittata, page 86

Roasted Red Pepper Dip

This dip thickens when refrigerated for several hours. Perfect to serve with vegetables. Makes 2¹/₂cups (625 mL).

Large red pepper	1	1
Garlic cloves, skin left on	3	3
Non-fat sour cream	1 cup	250 mL
Yogurt Cheese, page 67	1 cup	250 mL
Granulated sugar	1 tbsp.	15 mL
Chopped fresh sweet basil	2 tsp.	10 mL

Place red pepper and garlic cloves on broiler pan. Broil 4 inches from heat, turning occasionally, until pepper is completely blackened. ■ Place red pepper and garlic into paper bag or plastic bag to cool. ■ Peel red pepper and garlic. Place in blender. Add sour cream, yogurt cheese, sugar and basil. Process until red pepper and garlic are finely chopped. Refrigerate for several hours.

Nutrition Information

2 tbsp. (30 mL): 20 Calories; 2 g Protein; trace Total Fat (trace Sat., 0.5 mg Cholesterol); 23 mg Sodium

1. Bean And Vegetable Soup, page 138
2. Orzo Mushroom Soup, page 138
3. Thai Chicken In Rice Crust, page 76
4. Fajita Sandwiches, page 75
5. Comfort Corn Chowder, page 139
6. Roasted Onion And Garlic Bisque, page 140

Sunny Tomato Spread

Serve with vegetables, crackers or bread. Makes 1 cup (250 mL). Pictured on page 17.

Dry curd cottage cheese	1 cup	250 mL
1% buttermilk	1/2 cup	125 mL
Chopped fresh sweet basil	1/4 cup	60 mL
Garlic clove, crushed	1	1
Finely chopped toasted pine nuts	1 tbsp.	15 mL
Sun-dried tomato halves, softened in boiling water for 10 minutes	6	6
Grated fresh Parmesan cheese	1 tbsp.	15 mL

Combine cottage cheese, buttermilk, basil, garlic and pine nuts in blender. Process until smooth. ■ Add tomato and Parmesan cheese. Process until tomato is finely chopped. Chill for several hours before serving.

Nutrition Information

2 tbsp. (30 mL): 50 Calories; 6 g Protein; 1.2 g Total Fat (0.4 g Sat., 2.9 mg Cholesterol); 35 mg Sodium

Skinny Dilly Dip

Store in the refrigerator for three to four days. Makes 1 1/2 cups (375 mL).

Non-fat sour cream	1 cup	250 mL
Yogurt Cheese, page 67	1/2 cup	125 mL
Dill weed	1 tbsp.	15 mL
Onion powder (optional)	1/4 tsp.	1 mL
Salt	1/4 tsp.	1 mL
White pepper	1/8 tsp.	0.5 mL

Combine all 6 ingredients in medium bowl. Whisk until smooth. Chill in refrigerator for at least 1 hour.

Nutrition Information

2 tbsp. (30 mL): 14 Calories; 1 g Protein; trace Total Fat (trace Sat., 0.3 mg Cholesterol); 69 mg Sodium

Luncheon Fare

When dinner is light, or when you are just looking for something different for lunch, take a look at these great recipes. Sandwiches, pizzas and patties are a sample of what's in store. Get creative the next time you are thinking of making a sandwich—try one of these.

Fajita Sandwiches

Serve with fresh fruit for a simple week-night meal. Makes 6 buns. Pictured on page 72.

Lean ground chicken or turkey	1 lb.	454 g
Garlic cloves, minced	2	2
Lime juice, fresh or bottled	1 tbsp.	15 mL
Dried crushed chilies	$1/_4$ tsp.	1 mL
Low-sodium soy sauce	2 tsp.	10 mL
Paprika	$1/_4$ tsp.	1 mL
Salt	$1/_2$ tsp.	2 mL
Sweet onion, sliced into $1/_2$ inch (12 mm) slices	1	1
Red pepper, cut into thin slivers	1	1
Yellow pepper, cut into thin slivers	1	1
Lime juice, fresh or bottled	1 tbsp.	15 mL
Low-sodium soy sauce	1 tbsp.	15 mL
Granulated sugar	1 tsp.	5 mL
Ground coriander	$1/_4$ tsp.	1 mL
Freshly ground pepper	$1/_4$ tsp.	1 mL
Salsa, mild or medium	$1/_2$ cup	125 mL
Crusty buns	6	6

Lightly grease non-stick skillet or wok. Sauté chicken with garlic for 3 to 4 minutes. Add first amount of lime juice, chilies, soy sauce, paprika and salt. Sauté for 4 to 5 minutes until chicken is opaque. ■ Add onion, peppers, second amount of lime juice, soy sauce, sugar, coriander and pepper. Stir-fry for 4 to 5 minutes until vegetables are tender and chicken is cooked. Add salsa. Stir until hot. Remove from heat. ■ Cut buns in half and remove just a bit of soft center from each bun. Fill 6 halves with $3/_4$ to 1 cup (175 to 250 mL) fajita mixture and top with other half bun.

Nutrition Information

1 bun: 279 Calories; 22 g Protein; 3.8 g Total Fat (0.9 g Sat., 50.7 mg Cholesterol); 1097 mg Sodium

Thai Chicken In Rice Crust

A hint of red wine vinegar is behind the peanut butter taste. Prepare this as an alternative to the usual pizza. Makes 8 wedges. Pictured on page 72.

RICE CRUST		
Cooked brown rice	3 cups	750 mL
Egg whites (large), fork-beaten	3	3
Chopped fresh mint	1/4 cup	60 mL
THAI PEANUT SPREAD		
Smooth peanut butter	2 tbsp.	30 mL
Non-fat spreadable cream cheese	1/2 cup	125 mL
Sesame oil	1 tsp.	5 mL
Cayenne pepper	1/8 tsp.	0.5 mL
Dried crushed chilies	1/8 tsp.	0.5 mL
Low-sodium soy sauce	2 tsp.	10 mL
Red wine vinegar	1 tbsp.	15 mL
Granulated sugar	1/2 tsp.	2 mL
Boneless, skinless chicken breast halves, cut into slivers	2	2
Chili oil	1 tsp.	5 mL
Carrots, cut julienne	2	2
Low-sodium soy sauce	1 tbsp.	15 mL
Dried crushed chilies	1/8 tsp.	0.5 mL
Green onions, halved lengthwise and cut into 2 inch (5 cm) lengths	4	4
Tomato sauce	2 tbsp.	30 mL
Grated part-skim mozzarella cheese	1/2 cup	125 mL
Fresh bean sprouts	3 cups	750 mL
Sesame seeds	1 tbsp.	15 mL
Green onion, sliced	1	1

Rice Crust: Stir all 3 ingredients together in medium bowl. Pack evenly and firmly into lightly greased 12 inch (30 cm) pizza pan. Bake in 350°F (175°C) oven for 5 minutes just to firm crust. Cool slightly. ■ **Thai Peanut Spread:** Stir all 8 ingredients together in small bowl. Spread over crust. ■ Sauté chicken in chili oil in non-stick skillet. Toss for 3 minutes. Add carrot and toss for another 2 minutes. Add soy sauce, second amount of dried chilies, first amount of green onion and tomato sauce. Heat and stir until well combined and dry. Spread over peanut sauce. ■ Sprinkle with cheese. Bake in 400°F (205°C) oven on center rack for 7 minutes. ■ Sprinkle with bean sprouts, sesame seeds and second amount of green onion. Bake for 5 minutes.

Nutrition Information

1 wedge: 226 Calories; 16 g Protein; 6.2 g Total Fat (1.6 g Sat., 21.5 mg Cholesterol); 265 mg Sodium

Chicken Fajitas

Preparation time is 25 minutes. A fun meal to eat with your hands. Makes 6 fajitas.
Pictured on page 71.

Condensed chicken broth (10 oz., 284 mL)	$^1/_4$ **cup**	**60 mL**
Lime juice, fresh or bottled	$^1/_4$ **cup**	**60 mL**
Garlic cloves, crushed	**2**	**2**
Dried crushed chilies	$^1/_2$ **tsp.**	**2 mL**
Chili powder	$^1/_2$ **tsp.**	**2 mL**
Ground cumin (optional)	$^1/_8$ **tsp.**	**0.5 mL**
Boneless, skinless chicken breast halves	**3**	**3**
Large onion, thinly sliced into rings	**1**	**1**
Red pepper, thinly sliced	**1**	**1**
Green pepper, thinly sliced	**1**	**1**
Flour tortillas, 9 inch (22 cm)	**6**	**6**
Non-fat sour cream (optional)		
Shredded lettuce (optional)		
Diced tomatoes (optional)		

Combine first 6 ingredients in medium bowl. ■ Add chicken. Turn to coat. Marinate while preparing vegetables. Heat lightly greased large non-stick skillet until hot. Remove chicken from marinade. Reserve marinade. Sear chicken in skillet until browned. ■ Add onion, peppers and reserved marinade. Toss together. Cover and cook for 7 minutes until vegetables are tender and chicken is cooked. Remove chicken to cutting board and slice thinly. ■ Stack 6 tortillas and wrap in damp, clean tea towel. Gently warm in microwave or warm oven. Place about $^2/_3$ cup (150 mL) chicken and vegetables down center of each tortilla. Add sour cream, lettuce and tomatoes as desired. Fold both sides over center.

Nutrition Information

1 fajita: 252 Calories; 20 g Protein; 1.8 g Total Fat (0.4 g Sat., 34.3 mg Cholesterol); 318 mg Sodium

....

Use lean or extra lean ground beef. Extra lean contains less than 10% fat; lean contains less than 17% fat; regular contains less than 30% fat.

Polenta Wedges

The secret to a successful polenta is to stir it constantly until very thick. You will need strong arms. Serve as a main course with Creamy Dijon Spinach Sauce, page 134, or Three Tomato Sauce, page 132. Cuts into 8 wedges. Pictured on page 71.

Condensed chicken broth	**10 oz.**	**284 mL**
Water	**4³/₄ cups**	**1.2 L**
Cornmeal	**1¹/₂ cups**	**375 mL**
Grated light Parmesan cheese	**¹/₄ cup**	**60 mL**
Oregano or Italian spice	**¹/₂ tsp.**	**2 mL**
Chopped fresh parsley	**¹/₄ cup**	**60 mL**
Finely diced pimiento, drained, or roasted red pepper	**2 tbsp.**	**30 mL**
Grated light Parmesan cheese product	**1 tbsp.**	**15 mL**

Bring broth and water to a boil in non-stick skillet. Add cornmeal slowly, stirring constantly with whisk for about 25 minutes, until mixture is very thick and leaves sides of pan. ■ Stir in first amount of Parmesan cheese, oregano, parsley and pimiento during last 5 minutes of cooking. Pour into lightly greased 9 inch (22 cm) pie plate. Spread polenta evenly. Cover with plastic wrap and let cool until firm. ■ Remove polenta from pie plate to cutting board. Cut evenly into 8 wedges. Place wedges on foil-lined baking sheet. Lightly grease top of polenta and sprinkle with second amount of Parmesan cheese. Broil on center rack in oven for about 10 minutes until warm and golden on surface.

Nutrition Information

1 wedge: 126 Calories; 6 g Protein; 1.5 g Total Fat (0.6 g Sat., 2 mg Cholesterol); 311 mg Sodium

 Scramble-fry ground meats in a non-stick skillet without added fat, then drain off any excess fat.

Lentil Cakes With Mushroom Topping

The topping is best served immediately. The lentil cakes can be refrigerated or frozen and reheated when desired. Makes 17 lentil cakes and 2 cups (500 mL) topping. Pictured on page 126.

Lentils, any color	$^3/_4$ **cup**	175 mL
Water	**3 cups**	750 mL
Whole wheat flour	$^3/_4$ **cup**	175 mL
All-purpose flour	$^3/_4$ **cup**	175 mL
Baking powder	**4 tsp.**	20 mL
Crushed caraway seed	$^1/_2$ **tsp.**	2 mL
Grated light Parmesan cheese	**2 tbsp.**	30 mL
Egg whites (large), fork-beaten	**3**	3
Canola oil or vegetable oil	**2 tbsp.**	30 mL
Skim milk	**1$^1/_4$ cups**	300 mL
Salt	$^1/_2$ **tsp.**	2 mL
MUSHROOM TOPPING		
Red pepper, seeded and quartered	**1**	1
Medium red onion, quartered	**1**	1
Portabello mushroom slices	**6**	6
Olive oil (or use cooking spray)	**1 tsp.**	5 mL
Grated lemon peel	$^1/_2$ **tsp.**	2 mL
Freshly ground pepper, sprinkle		
Seasoning salt	$^1/_2$ **tsp.**	2 mL
Grated light Parmesan cheese product	**1 tbsp.**	15 mL

Boil lentils in water in large saucepan for about 5 minutes until just tender. Drain. ■ Stir both flours, baking powder, caraway seed and Parmesan cheese together in medium bowl. Add lentils and toss together. ■ Beat egg whites on medium until soft peaks form. Add oil, milk and salt. Stir egg white mixture into lentil mixture and stir until quite smooth. Grease non-stick skillet. Heat on medium until hot. Drop lentil batter by spoonfuls onto hot pan and cook as for pancakes. ■ **Mushroom Topping:** Lay red pepper, onion and mushroom slices on baking sheet with sides. Lightly brush all vegetables with olive oil. Bake in 500°F (260°C) oven on highest rack for 20 minutes until vegetables are tender. Let cool on baking sheet. Dice all vegetables into medium bowl and pour in any leftover juices from baking sheet. Stir in lemon peel, pepper, salt and cheese.

Nutrition Information

1 lentil cake with 2 tbsp. (30 mL) topping: 108 Calories; 6 g Protein; 4.8 g Total Fat (0.4 g Sat., 0.8 mg Cholesterol); 205 mg Sodium

Falafel Pizza

Falafels are a Middle Eastern specialty. This is quite a tasty variation of falafels. Cuts into 8 wedges. Pictured on page 126.

All-purpose flour	1¹/₂ cups	375 mL
Whole wheat flour	1 cup	250 mL
Instant yeast	2 tsp.	10 mL
Salt	¹/₄ tsp.	1 mL
Granulated sugar	2 tsp.	10 mL
Toasted sesame seeds	2 tbsp.	30 mL
Hot water	1 cup	250 mL
Olive oil	2 tbsp.	30 mL
Chicken bouillon powder	¹/₂ tsp.	2 mL
Boiling water	¹/₂ cup	125 mL
Chopped onion	1 cup	250 mL
Garlic cloves, minced	3	3
Canned chick peas (garbanzo beans), drained	19 oz.	540 mL
Egg white (large)	1	1
Chopped fresh parsley	1¹/₂ tbsp.	25 mL
Ground cumin	¹/₂ tsp.	2 mL
Ground coriander	³/₄ tsp.	4 mL
Ground turmeric	¹/₈ tsp.	0.5 mL
Salt	1 tsp.	5 mL
Freshly ground pepper	¹/₈ tsp.	0.5 mL
Thin tomato slices	12	12
Thin green pepper rings	12	12
Thin red onion rings	12	12
Grated part-skim mozzarella cheese	1 cup	250 mL

Combine first 6 ingredients in medium bowl. Stir water and oil together in small cup. Add all at once to flour mixture, stirring with fork until combined and dough leaves sides of bowl. Turn out on lightly floured surface and knead about 30 times. Cover with bowl. Allow to rest for 10 minutes. ■ Dissolve bouillon powder in boiling water in small saucepan. Stir well. Cook onion and garlic in broth for 7 to 8 minutes until soft. ■ Put next 8 ingredients into food processor. Process to combine. Add broth mixture and process until almost smooth. ■ Lightly grease flat working surface. Roll out dough to fit 14 inch (35 cm) pizza pan. Lightly grease pizza pan and fit dough in, making slightly raised edge all around. Spread chick pea mixture over crust. Bake in 425°F (220°C) oven, on center rack for 15 minutes. Top with tomato slices, pepper rings and red onion rings. Sprinkle with mozzarella cheese. Bake for 15 minutes until cheese is lightly browned.

Nutrition Information

1 wedge: 305 Calories; 13 g Protein; 8.5 g Total Fat (2.4 g Sat., 8.9 mg Cholesterol); 621 mg Sodium

Wrapped Salad Loaf

This sandwich is very refreshing. The combination of vegetables creates the perfect taste. Great for a lunch or light dinner. Cuts into 6 sandwiches. Pictured on page 125.

Plum tomatoes, seeded and cut julienne	2	2
Finely chopped ripe pitted olives	2 tbsp.	30 mL
Chopped fresh sweet basil	2 tbsp.	30 mL
Salt	$^1/_4$ tsp.	1 mL
Freshly ground pepper, sprinkle		
Olive oil	1 tbsp.	15 mL
Red wine vinegar	1 tbsp.	15 mL
English cucumber, 6 inch (15 cm) length, with peel	1	1
Red, yellow or green bell pepper	1	1
Multi-grain baguette, 20 inch (50 cm) length	1	1
Red onion, sliced lengthwise paper-thin	$^1/_2$	$^1/_2$
Mixed sprouts	1 cup	250 mL

Toss tomatoes and olives with basil, vinegar, salt and pepper in small bowl. Drizzle with olive oil and vinegar. Gently stir to combine. Let stand at room temperature while preparing vegetables and bread. ■ Slice cucumber and pepper in half lengthwise into long slivers. ■ Cut baguette in half lengthwise. Gently remove enough of insides to make slight depression on both sides. Drain tomato mixture, reserving juices. Brush reserved juice over insides of both halves of bread. Layer cucumber, pepper, onion and sprouts evenly over surface of one half of bread. Cover with second half of bread. Slice diagonally into 6 sandwiches. Wrap tightly in plastic wrap if not using immediately and store in refrigerator.

Nutrition Information

1 sandwich: 140 Calories; 5 g Protein; 3.7 g Total Fat (0.6 g Sat., 0 mg Cholesterol); 333 mg Sodium

Variation: Sprinkle with $^1/_2$ cup (125 mL) grated cheese (your favorite) just before covering with second half of bread.

....

Select tuna packed in water, not in oil. If packed in oil, rinse under hot water to remove most of the fat.

Foo Yong Omelet

A light main course or luncheon for four. Smaller pancake-size omelets can also be made instead of two larger omelets. Makes 8 wedges.

Grated carrot	**¹/₄ cup**	**60 mL**
Chopped onion	**¹/₂ cup**	**125 mL**
Chopped celery	**¹/₂ cup**	**125 mL**
Small garlic clove, crushed	**1**	**1**
Fresh bean sprouts	**2 cups**	**500 mL**
Frozen egg product (such as Egg Beaters), thawed	**1 cup**	**250 mL**
Salt, sprinkle		
Pepper, sprinkle		
SAUCE		
Condensed chicken broth (10 oz., 284 mL)	**¹/₄ cup**	**60 mL**
Water	**¹/₄ cup**	**60 mL**
Low-sodium soy sauce	**4 tsp.**	**20 mL**
Cornstarch	**1¹/₂ tsp.**	**7 mL**

Lightly grease 10 inch (25 cm) non-stick skillet. Sauté carrot, onion, celery, garlic and bean sprouts for 5 minutes. Remove to bowl. ■ Lightly grease skillet again and pour in ¹/₂ cup (125 mL) egg product. Sprinkle with salt and pepper. Spread half of vegetables over top of egg. Cover. Cook about 3 minutes, without stirring, until firm enough to flip over. Turn over and cook for 1 minute. Remove to platter and keep warm. Repeat with remaining egg product and vegetables. Cut each omelet into 4 wedges. ■ **Sauce:** Combine all 4 ingredients in small saucepan. Heat, while stirring, until sauce is boiling and slightly thickened. Drizzle sauce over wedges to serve, or serve sauce separately on the side.

Nutrition Information

1 wedge: 39 Calories; 5 g Protein; 0.4 g Total Fat (0.1 g Sat., 0.1 mg Cholesterol); 297 mg Sodium

Substitute ¹/₄ cup (60 mL) frozen egg product (such as Egg Beaters) for each large egg in a recipe.

Roasted Vegetable Focaccia

So eye-catching! So delicious! So easy! Only 30 minutes from start to finish. Cuts into 8 large wedges. Pictured on page 71.

Medium red onion, thinly sliced	1/2	1/2
Sliced fresh mushrooms	2 cups	500 mL
Yellow or orange bell pepper, cut into slivers	1	1
Plum tomatoes, chopped	2	2
Olive oil	1/2 tsp.	2 mL
Balsamic vinegar	2 tbsp.	30 mL
Small garlic clove, crushed	1	1
Chopped fresh basil	2 tbsp.	30 mL
Freshly ground pepper	1/4 tsp.	1 mL
Thin crust Italian focaccia or flatbread, 12 inch (30 cm)	1	1
Grated part-skim mozzarella cheese	1 cup	250 mL

Combine all 4 vegetables in large bowl. ■ Measure oil, vinegar, garlic, basil and pepper into small bowl. Whisk together well. Pour over vegetables. Toss together. Place vegetables in single layer on large ungreased baking sheet with sides. Bake, uncovered, in 500°F (260°C) oven on top rack for 10 minutes until vegetables are tender. ■ Reduce heat to 450°F (230°C). Arrange roasted vegetables evenly on focaccia, spreading to edges. Sprinkle with cheese. Place focaccia in large pizza pan or directly onto rack in center of oven and bake for 8 to 10 minutes until cheese is melted and crust is crispy.

Nutrition Information

1 wedge: 168 Calories; 8 g Protein; 3.8 g Total Fat (1.8 g Sat., 9.7 mg Cholesterol); 546 mg Sodium

Select breads, cereals and crackers that are low in fat. For example, choose bagels instead of croissants.

Beef Stroganoff

Partially freeze the steak for easier slicing. Serve over whole wheat pasta, brown rice, tomato pasta or yellow (carrot) pasta. Makes 4 cups (1 L).

Lean top sirloin steak, trimmed of all visible fat	1 lb.	454 g
Medium onions, thinly sliced	2	2
Garlic cloves, crushed	2	2
Sliced fresh mushrooms	3 cups	750 mL
Condensed beef broth	10 oz.	284 mL
Worcestershire sauce	1 tsp.	5 mL
Skim evaporated milk	13$\frac{1}{2}$ oz.	385 mL
Cornstarch	2 tbsp.	30 mL
Non-fat sour cream	1 cup	250 mL
Salt	1 tsp.	5 mL
Pepper	$\frac{1}{4}$ tsp.	1 mL

Cut steak across grain into very thin slices. Lightly grease large non-stick skillet or wok. Sauté onion, garlic and mushrooms until vegetables are tender and all liquid is evaporated. Add steak. Sauté for 6 minutes. ■ Stir in broth and Worcestershire sauce. Combine milk with cornstarch in small cup. Stir into meat mixture in skillet. Heat until mixture boils and thickens. Remove from heat and stir in sour cream. Season with salt and pepper.

Nutrition Information

1 cup (250 mL): 294 Calories; 36 g Protein; 5 g Total Fat (1.9 g Sat., 57.2 mg Cholesterol); 1363 mg Sodium

Turkey Apple Burgers

These are quick to make and easy to assemble. Makes 6 burgers. Pictured on page 126.

Lean ground turkey	1 lb.	454 g
Large egg, fork-beaten	1	1
Finely crushed soda crackers	1 cup	250 mL
Finely chopped onion	2 tbsp.	30 mL
Small garlic clove, crushed	1	1
Red apple, with peel, finely diced	1	1
Chopped fresh parsley	1 tbsp.	15 mL
Salt	$\frac{3}{4}$ tsp.	4 mL
Pepper	$\frac{1}{2}$ tsp.	2 mL

(continued on next page)

Combine all 9 ingredients in large bowl. Form into 6 patties. Broil 4 inches (10 cm) from heat for 10 minutes per side, or grill over medium heat on barbecue.

1 burger: 174 Calories; 19 g Protein; 4 g Total Fat (1.1 g Sat., 91.2 mg Cholesterol); 552 mg Sodium

Curried Shrimp With Couscous

Mellow curry flavor with slight sweetness from the chutney. The yogurt helps to "cool" the dish. Serves 6. Pictured on page 76.

Low-fat chicken bouillon cube	$^1/_4 \times ^1/_3$ **oz.**	$^1/_4 \times$ **10.5g**
Boiling water	$^1/_4$ **cup**	**60 mL**
Fresh Mango Chutney, page 136	$^1/_3$ **cup**	**75 mL**
Curry paste (available in Oriental section of grocery store)	**1 tbsp.**	**15 mL**
Carrots, thinly sliced on the diagonal	**3**	**3**
Medium onion, halved lengthwise and slivered	**1**	**1**
Red pepper, cut into 1 inch (2.5 cm) pieces	**1**	**1**
Fresh shelled peas or pea pods	**1 cup**	**250 mL**
Cooked medium-large fresh shrimp, peeled and deveined	**1 lb.**	**454 g**
Non-fat plain yogurt	$^3/_4$ **cup**	**175 mL**
Boiling water	**1$^1/_2$ cups**	**375 mL**
Couscous	**1$^1/_2$ cups**	**375 mL**

Dissolve partial bouillon cube in water to make broth. Stir well. ■ Heat broth, chutney and curry paste in non-stick wok. Add carrot and onion. Stir-fry for 3 minutes. Add red pepper and peas. Toss together and stir-fry for 3 minutes until pepper is tender-crisp and peas are bright green. Add shrimp. Cover. Toss for 2 minutes until heated through. Remove from heat. Stir in yogurt. ■ Pour boiling water over couscous. Let stand for 5 minutes. Serve shrimp mixture over top.

1 serving: 338 Calories; 25 g Protein; 2.5 g Total Fat (0.4 g Sat., 115.6 mg Cholesterol); 257 mg Sodium

Add flavor, texture and color to a sandwich with fresh vegetables, sprouts, sliced fresh fruit or roasted peppers.

Shrimp Frittata

Make this for brunch, lunch or dinner. Serves 6. Pictured on page 71.

Day old bread slices	6	6
Cooked small shrimp	8 oz.	225 g
Grated low-fat Cheddar cheese	1/2 cup	125 mL
Finely diced red or green pepper	1/4 cup	60 mL
Frozen egg product (such as Egg Beaters), thawed	1 cup	250 mL
Dijon mustard	2 tsp.	10 mL
Celery salt	1/2 tsp.	2 mL
Skim evaporated milk	13 1/2 oz.	385 mL
Skim milk	1/3 cup	75 mL
Crisp rice cereal (such as Special K)	1/2 cup	125 mL
Grated low-fat Cheddar cheese	1/2 cup	125 mL
Paprika, sprinkle		

Cut bread slices into 1/2 inch (12 mm) cubes. Lightly grease 9 inch (22 cm) round glass baking dish or 2 quart (2 L) casserole dish. Place half of bread cubes in bottom of dish. Sprinkle with shrimp, first amount of cheese and all of peppers. Top with remaining bread cubes. ■ Combine egg product, mustard, celery salt and both milks in medium bowl. Pour over casserole, pressing down lightly. Bake, uncovered, in 350°F (175°C) oven for 45 minutes. ■ Combine cereal and second amount of cheese. Spread over casserole. Sprinkle with paprika. Bake, uncovered, for 15 minutes until cheese is melted. Let stand for 5 minutes before serving.

Nutrition Information

1 serving: 265 Calories; 26 g Protein; 5.9 g Total Fat (3 g Sat., 88.7 mg Cholesterol); 678 mg Sodium

Use skim evaporated milk instead of cream. By comparison, 1/2 cup (125 mL) of skim evaporated milk contains 0.3 grams of fat; cereal cream (half & half) contains almost 13 grams; and regular table cream (coffee cream) contains from 19 to 23 grams.

Main Courses

I f you are wondering about what to make for dinner, take your pick from this wide variety of delicious, low-fat main course recipes. You can't go wrong! From skinless chicken breasts and fish fillets to lean cuts of beef and pork, your family will be thrilled to try the great flavors of low-fat cooking!

Turkey Roast With Cranberry Rhubarb Sauce

Enough white meat for everyone! Less roasting time than a whole bird. Serves 8.

CRANBERRY RHUBARB SAUCE		
Chopped rhubarb, fresh or frozen	2 cups	500 mL
Cranberries, fresh or frozen	2 cups	500 mL
Granulated sugar	$^1/_2$ cup	125 mL
Cinnamon stick, 4 inches (10 cm) long	1	1
Juice and grated peel of 1 orange		
Cointreau or other orange liqueur	2 tbsp.	30 mL
Turkey breast roast, boned and tied	$3^1/_3$ lbs.	1.5 kg

Cranberry Rhubarb Sauce: Combine rhubarb and cranberries with sugar, cinnamon, orange juice and peel in medium saucepan. Bring to a boil. Reduce heat immediately. Cover and simmer for 6 minutes until cranberries start to burst. Remove from heat. Cool slightly. Remove cinnamon stick. Stir in Cointreau. ■ Place turkey in ungreased 3 quart (3 L) casserole dish. Spread $^1/_2$ cup (125 mL) sauce over top. Roast, covered, in 350°F (175°C) oven for 40 minutes, basting with pan juices at half time. Spread another $^1/_2$ cup (125 mL) sauce over top. Roast, covered, for 40 to 50 minutes, basting with pan juices at half time. Insert meat thermometer. It should register 170°F (75°C). Scrape off and discard rhubarb and cranberry coating from roast. Discard basting juices. Slice turkey and serve with remaining 2 cups (500 mL) sauce.

Nutrition Information

1 serving: 295 Calories; 47 g Protein; 1.4 g Total Fat (0.4 g Sat., 116.3 mg Cholesterol); 93 mg Sodium

Teriyaki Chicken

Preparation time is only 10 minutes. Serve with rice and Fresh Mango Chutney, page 136. Makes 1²/₃ cups (400 mL) sauce with about 12 pieces of chicken. Serves 6.

Skinless, bone-in chicken parts	**3 lbs.**	**1.4 kg**
Fresh lemon juice	**1 tbsp.**	**15 mL**
Grated lemon peel	**1 tsp.**	**5 mL**
Garlic cloves, minced	**3**	**3**
Sherry (or alcohol-free sherry)	**¹/₄ cup**	**60 mL**
Brown sugar, packed	**¹/₂ cup**	**125 mL**
Mild molasses	**2 tbsp.**	**30 mL**
Dijon mustard	**1 tbsp.**	**15 mL**
Low-sodium soy sauce	**¹/₄ cup**	**60 mL**
Hot pepper sauce	**¹/₈ tsp.**	**0.5 mL**
Cornstarch	**4 tsp.**	**20 mL**

Lightly grease shallow roasting pan. Place chicken parts in single layer on bottom.
■ Combine remaining 10 ingredients in small bowl. Mix well. Pour over chicken. Bake, covered, in 350°F (175°C) oven for 45 minutes. Remove lid. Turn chicken over. Bake, uncovered, for 15 minutes.

Nutrition Information

1 serving: 250 Calories; 26 g Protein; 3.4 g Total Fat (0.8 g Sat., 77.4 mg Cholesterol); 570 mg Sodium

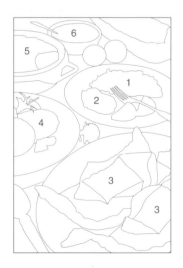

Apricot Chicken

This will go perfectly with a green salad. This only takes 15 minutes to prepare. Serves 6.
Pictured on page 89.

Canned apricot halves, in juice	**14 oz.**	**398 mL**
Grated gingerroot	**$^1/_2$ tsp.**	**2 mL**
Chili sauce	**2 tbsp.**	**30 mL**
Liquid honey	**3 tbsp.**	**50 mL**
Low-sodium soy sauce	**1 tbsp.**	**15 mL**
Boneless, skinless chicken breast halves	**6**	**6**

Drain apricot juice into small bowl and set fruit aside. Add gingerroot, chili sauce, honey and soy sauce to juice. Stir well. ■ Place chicken and juice mixture in sealable plastic bag. Marinate for a few hours or overnight in refrigerator, turning to coat. Lightly grease 2 quart (2 L) casserole dish. Lay chicken in bottom. Bake in 350°F (175°C) oven for 20 minutes. Pour marinade into small saucepan and boil for 4 minutes to slightly reduce and thicken sauce. Brush some sauce over chicken and bake for 20 minutes. Arrange reserved apricot halves over chicken. Drizzle remaining sauce over all and bake for 10 minutes until apricots are hot.

Nutrition Information

1 serving: 203 Calories; 28 g Protein; 1.5 g Total Fat (0.4 g Sat.,68.4 mg Cholesterol); 331 mg Sodium

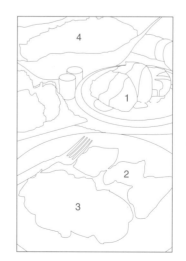

1. Rolled Turkey And Stuffing With Wine Sauce, page 94
2. Tomato Sherry Chicken, page 95
3. Antipasto Salad, page 120
4. Mixed Vegetable Wok, page 150

Far East Chicken

A great combination with couscous or rice pilaf. Serves 8.

Skinless, bone-in chicken breast halves and thighs	**4 lbs.**	**1.8 kg**
Small onion, coarsely chopped	**1**	**1**
Plain skim milk yogurt	**2 cups**	**500 mL**
Lime juice, fresh or bottled	**¹/₄ cup**	**60 mL**
Garlic cloves, crushed	**3**	**3**
Grated gingerroot	**1 tbsp.**	**15 mL**
Ground turmeric	**¹/₂ tsp.**	**2 mL**
Ground cumin	**¹/₄ tsp.**	**1 mL**
Ground coriander	**¹/₂ tsp.**	**2 mL**
Ground cardamom	**¹/₂ tsp.**	**2 mL**
Paprika	**2 tsp.**	**10 mL**
Salt	**2 tsp.**	**10 mL**

Wash chicken. Pat dry and score in several places with sharp knife. Place in large glass or non-metal bowl or in extra large freezer bag. ■ Combine remaining 11 ingredients in medium bowl and pour over chicken. Stir well so all chicken pieces are coated. Marinate for 12 to 24 hours in refrigerator, stirring to re-coat chicken pieces several times. Remove chicken from yogurt mixture and discard marinade. Arrange chicken pieces in ungreased 9 × 13 inch (22 × 33 cm) baking dish. Bake in 375°F (190°C) oven for 1 hour or until no longer pink in thickest pieces of chicken.

Variation: Barbecue marinated chicken on greased grill over medium-low heat for about 1 hour. Turn frequently to brown and cook throughout.

Nutrition Information

1 serving: 181 Calories; 32 g Protein; 3.2 g Total Fat (0.8 g Sat., 94.9 mg Cholesterol); 465 mg Sodium

Choose fish, poultry (with skin and visible fat removed) or lean cuts of meat. The more tender cuts of meat contain more fat, so plan a smaller portion per serving.

Cornmeal Chicken With Fresh Tomato Sauce

The flavor of the sauce intensifies as it stands. Prepare the tomato sauce while the chicken is being baked. Serves 6. Pictured on page 18.

Boneless, skinless chicken breast halves	6	6
Egg whites (large), fork-beaten	2	2
Cornmeal	$^1/_2$ **cup**	125 mL
Chili powder	2 tsp.	10 mL
Dried oregano, crushed	1 tsp.	5 mL
Seasoning salt	$^1/_2$ tsp.	2 mL
Cooking spray, for crispness (optional)		
FRESH TOMATO SAUCE		
Large plum tomatoes quartered	2	2
Green onions, sliced in large pieces	4	4
Small garlic clove	1	1
Small fresh chili pepper or jalapeño pepper	1	1
Chopped fresh cilantro	1 tbsp.	15 mL
Lime juice, fresh or bottled	2 tsp.	10 mL
Salt	$^1/_2$ tsp.	2 mL

Wash chicken and pat dry with paper towel. Cut each chicken breast half in half diagonally to make 12 long, narrow pieces. ■ Toss chicken with egg whites in medium bowl. ■ Lightly grease shallow baking sheet with sides. Mix cornmeal, chili powder, oregano and seasoning salt in small bowl. Sprinkle $^1/_2$ cornmeal mixture on sheet of waxed paper. Roll $^1/_2$ chicken pieces in cornmeal to lightly coat. Arrange coated chicken on baking sheet. Repeat with other $^1/_2$ chicken pieces. Lightly oil surface of coated chicken with cooking spray. Bake in 350°F (175°C) oven for 15 minutes. Turn pieces over. Bake for 10 minutes until chicken is cooked and coating is golden. ■ **Fresh Tomato Sauce:** Process all 7 ingredients in food processor until almost puréed. Flavor intensifies if left to stand. Serve with chicken.

Nutrition Information

1 serving: 197 Calories; 30 g Protein; 2 g Total Fat (0.4 g Sat., 68.4 mg Cholesterol); 561 mg Sodium

Trim all visible fat from beef, chicken and pork. Remove the skin from poultry.

Rolled Turkey And Stuffing With Wine Sauce

A bit fussy to make but it's not difficult. The end result is delicious and very attractive when served already sliced. Drizzle some of the sauce over the slices and serve the remaining sauce on the side. Serves 8. Pictured on page 90.

Chopped onion	1 cup	250 mL
Chopped celery	1 cup	250 mL
Hard margarine	1 tbsp.	15 mL
Grated carrot	1 cup	250 mL
Fine dry bread crumbs	1 cup	250 mL
Low-fat chicken bouillon cube	1 × $^1/_3$ oz.	1 × 10.5 g
Boiling water	$^3/_4$ cup	175 mL
Chopped fresh parsley	$^1/_4$ cup	60 mL
Ground sage	$^1/_2$ tsp.	2 mL
Ground thyme	$^1/_4$ tsp.	1 mL
Lean ground turkey	$1^1/_2$ lbs.	680 g
Egg whites (large), fork-beaten	2	2
Garlic clove, crushed	1	1
Fine dry bread crumbs	$^1/_4$ cup	60 mL
Salt	1 tsp.	5 mL
Pepper	1 tsp.	5 mL
Water	$^1/_2$ cup	125 mL
White wine	$^1/_2$ cup	125 mL
WINE SAUCE		
Pan drippings	$^1/_4$ cup	60 mL
White wine	$^1/_4$ cup	60 mL
Condensed chicken broth	10 oz.	284 mL
Cornstarch	2 tbsp.	30 mL
Water	$^1/_2$ cup	125 mL

Sauté onion and celery in margarine in non-stick skillet for 10 minutes. Add carrot. Sauté, stirring frequently, until onion is soft. Remove from heat and stir in first amount of bread crumbs. Dissolve bouillon cube in boiling water. Stir into onion mixture. Add parsley, sage and thyme. A handful squeezed together in your hand should hold its shape without falling apart. Add a bit of water if stuffing is still not moist enough. Set mixture aside. ■ Combine ground turkey with egg whites, garlic, second amount of bread crumbs, salt and pepper. Mix well. Lay out 16 inch (40 cm) long sheet of waxed paper. Spread turkey mixture evenly on waxed paper to form 10 × 14 inch (25 × 35 cm) rectangle, packing down to close any holes.

(continued on next page)

■ Cover meat with stuffing mixture and gently pat down with your hand. Roll up tightly from short side, removing waxed paper as you roll. Carefully place roll in lightly greased roaster. Bake, covered, in 350°F (175°C) oven for 1 hour. Pour in wine and water. Bake for $^1/_2$ hour, basting twice with juices. Remove roll to platter and let stand, tented with foil, while preparing sauce. ■ **Wine Sauce:** Strain drippings and skim off any fat. Combine with wine and condensed chicken broth. Mix cornstarch with water in small cup. Whisk into wine mixture. Heat until boiling and thickened. Makes $1^2/_3$ cups (400 mL) sauce.

Nutrition Information

1 serving with 3 tbsp. (50 mL) sauce: 239 Calories; 25 g Protein; 4.3 g Total Fat (1.1 g Sat., 62.6 mg Cholesterol); 889 mg Sodium

Tomato Sherry Chicken

The sauce has a slightly sweet flavor. Quite an elegant dish to serve to guests. Serves 4. Pictured on page 90 and on the front cover.

Olive oil	2 tsp.	10 mL
Boneless, skinless chicken breast halves, cut in half, lengthwise	4	4
Salt, sprinkle		
Freshly ground pepper, sprinkle		
Garlic clove, minced	1	1
Finely chopped shallots	$^1/_4$ cup	60 mL
Condensed chicken broth (10 oz., 284 mL)	1 cup	250 mL
Sun-dried tomato halves, quartered with scissors	8	8
Cornstarch	2 tsp.	10 mL
Sherry	$^1/_3$ cup	75 mL

Heat oil in large non-stick skillet on medium high. Sear chicken for 3 to 4 minutes on each side. Season with salt and pepper. Remove chicken to plate. Keep hot. ■ In remaining skillet juices, sauté garlic and shallots, stirring constantly, until just golden. Stir in chicken broth and bring to a boil. Add chicken, turning to coat in sauce. Simmer, covered, for 10 minutes, allowing chicken to finish cooking. ■ Remove cover. Remove chicken to plate. Keep warm. Stir in tomato. Simmer, stirring constantly, for 3 minutes. Combine cornstarch and sherry in small cup and stir into sauce. Simmer for about 2 minutes until sauce is slightly thickened and tomato is softened. Pour over chicken and serve.

Nutrition Information

1 serving: 228 Calories; 32 g Protein; 5 g Total Fat (1 g Sat., 69.2 mg Cholesterol); 562 mg Sodium

Stuffed Peppers

Preparation time is only 20 minutes. Use leftover brown rice or cook brown rice on the stove at the beginning before scramble-frying the ground chicken. Serves 6. Pictured on the front cover.

Ground chicken or turkey	¹/₂ **lb.**	**225 g**
Finely chopped onion	¹/₂ **cup**	**125 mL**
Finely diced celery	¹/₂ **cup**	**125 mL**
Garlic clove, minced	**1**	**1**
Cooked brown rice	**1**¹/₂ **cups**	**375 mL**
Tomato sauce	**7**¹/₂ **oz.**	**213 mL**
Granulated sugar	¹/₄ **tsp.**	**1 mL**
Whole oregano	¹/₄ **tsp.**	**1 mL**
Dried sweet basil	¹/₄ **tsp.**	**1 mL**
Salt	¹/₄ **tsp.**	**1 mL**
Freshly ground pepper	¹/₈ **tsp.**	**0.5 mL**
Large green, red or yellow peppers, halved lengthwise, seeds removed	**3**	**3**
Chicken bouillon powder	**1**¹/₂ **tsp.**	**7 mL**
Boiling water	¹/₄ **cup**	**60 mL**

Lightly grease non-stick skillet. Scramble-fry ground chicken, onion, celery and garlic for about 10 minutes until no pink remains in chicken and vegetables are tender.
■ Stir in rice, tomato sauce, sugar, oregano, basil, salt and pepper. Remove from heat.
■ Divide chicken mixture among pepper halves. Place in ungreased 9 x 13 inch (22 x 33 cm) baking dish. ■ Dissolve bouillon powder in water in small cup. Pour broth around peppers. Cover with foil. Bake in 350°F (175°C) oven for about 45 minutes. Peppers should remain tender-crisp.

Nutrition Information

1 serving: 131 Calories; 10 g Protein; 1.8 g Total Fat (0.4 g Sat., 24.5 mg Cholesterol); 539 mg Sodium

Bake, broil, grill, roast, stir-fry, braise or stew meats whenever possible, instead of frying in oil.

Crab-Stuffed Chicken With Parsley Sauce

A very appealing company dish. Leftovers can be refrigerated for up to three days and then reheated. Makes 6 chicken rolls. Pictured on page 144.

Boneless, skinless chicken breast halves	6	6
Canned crabmeat, drained, shredded and cartilage removed	4.2 oz.	120 g
Dry fine bread crumbs	1/4 cup	60 mL
Low-fat Cheddar cheese or Swiss cheese	1/4 cup	60 mL
Finely chopped red pepper	2 tbsp.	30 mL
White wine	3 tbsp.	50 mL
Salt, sprinkle		
Pepper, sprinkle		
Low-fat chicken bouillon cube	1/2 x 1/3 oz.	1/2 x 10.5 g
Boiling water	1/2 cup	125 mL
Bay leaf	1	1
Chopped fresh parsley	3 tbsp.	50 mL
Cornstarch	2 tsp.	10 mL
White wine	1 tbsp.	15 mL

Flatten chicken between 2 sheets of plastic wrap to 1/4 inch (6 mm), using flat side of mallet or rolling pin. ■ Combine crabmeat, crumbs, cheese and red pepper to make stuffing. Drizzle first amount of wine over chicken to moisten. Put 1/4 cup (60 mL) stuffing in middle of each piece and roll up starting on shorter side, tucking in sides to enclose stuffing. Fasten with wooden picks or tie with butchers' twine. Sprinkle rolls with salt and pepper. Place in ungreased 2 quart (2 L) casserole dish. ■ Dissolve partial bouillon cube in boiling water in small cup. Pour broth into casserole dish. Add bay leaf and sprinkle parsley over rolls. Bake, covered, in 350°F (175°C) oven for 45 minutes. Remove rolls to platter. Reserve liquid but discard bay leaf. ■ Heat reserved liquid on stove. Combine cornstarch and second amount of white wine in small cup. Slowly whisk into reserved liquid. Boil until slightly thickened. Remove wooden picks from rolls and pour sauce over to serve.

Nutrition Information

1 chicken roll: 190 Calories; 32 g Protein; 3 g Total Fat (1.1 g Sat., 81.5 mg Cholesterol); 438 mg Sodium

Spinach-Stuffed Sole

Ready in under one hour. The number of rolls will depend on the size of the fillets but you should get 6 larger or 9 smaller. Serves 6. Pictured on page 125.

Finely diced celery hearts and celery leaves	1/4 cup	60 mL
Finely diced onion	1/4 cup	60 mL
Olive oil	1 tsp.	5 mL
Packed chopped fresh spinach	1 cup	250 mL
Light spreadable cream cheese	1/4 cup	60 mL
Fine dry bread crumbs	1/2 cup	125 mL
Grated light Parmesan cheese product	2 tbsp.	30 mL
Lemon pepper	1/8 tsp.	0.5 mL
White wine	1 tbsp.	15 mL
Fresh sole fillets	1 lb.	454 g
SAUCE		
Light spreadable cream cheese	1/4 cup	60 mL
Skim evaporated milk	1/4 cup	60 mL
White wine	1 tbsp.	15 mL
Yogurt Cheese, page 67	1/2 cup	125 mL

Paprika, for garnish
Chopped fresh chives, for garnish

Sauté celery and onion in olive oil in non-stick skillet until onion is soft and clear. Stir in spinach. Sauté for 2 minutes until spinach is soft. Remove from heat. Stir in cream cheese until melted. Add bread crumbs, Parmesan cheese and lemon pepper. Stir in wine. Stuffing should hold together when squeezed. Add a bit more wine if needed.
■ Spread stuffing on top of each fillet. Roll up and secure with wooden pick. Lay, wooden pick side down, in lightly greased 1 1/2 quart (1.5 L) casserole dish. Cover. Bake in 350°F (175°C) oven for 15 to 20 minutes until fish flakes easily. Watch carefully, as rolls will split if overbaked. ■ **Sauce:** Combine cream cheese, evaporated milk and wine in small saucepan. Heat to melt cream cheese, stirring constantly. Simmer until smooth. Remove from heat. Stir in yogurt cheese. Makes 3/4 cup (175 mL) sauce. ■ Lay fish rolls on long platter. Pour sauce across top. Sprinkle with paprika and chives.

Nutrition Information

1 serving with 4 tsp. (20 mL) sauce: 203 Calories; 22 g Protein; 6 g Total Fat (2.6 g Sat., 49 mg Cholesterol); 426 mg Sodium

Gourmet Fish Steaks

It's a bit fussy to wrap and tie the spinach but it only takes 15 minutes to prepare. Make the sauce while the fish is baking. Serves 8. Pictured on page 144.

Spinach leaves, lightly steamed, approximately (see Note)	32	32
Firm fresh fish steaks (such as halibut), 1-1$^1/_4$ inch (2.5-3 cm) thick, (about 2 lbs., 900 g)	8	8
Olive oil	2 tsp.	10 mL
Salt, sprinkle		
Pepper, sprinkle		
Shallot, finely chopped	1	1
Lime juice, fresh or bottled	2 tbsp.	30 mL
Tequila	$^1/_3$ cup	75 mL
Pineapple juice	1 cup	250 mL

Pineapple spears (fresh or canned), for garnish

Fold limp spinach leaves lengthwise into 1 to 1$^1/_4$ inch (2.5 to 3 cm) wide strips. Wrap and press about 4 folded leaves around outside thickness of each fish steak. Tie butchers' string around circumference. ■ Heat olive oil in large non-stick skillet. Sear fish steaks for 2 minutes on each side until browned. Steaks should not be cooked completely. Season each browned side with salt and pepper. Remove to ovenproof plate or platter and place in 300°F (150°C) oven to finish cooking for 15 minutes while sauce is being prepared. ■ In same skillet, sauté shallot in oil and juices remaining in pan, until soft and golden. Pour in lime juice and tequila. Carefully ignite to burn off alcohol. Pour in pineapple juice. Boil for 5 to 6 minutes to reduce mixture to about half. ■ Remove fish steaks from oven. Remove string. Spoon sauce over all. Garnish with fresh pineapple spears.

Note: To steam spinach leaves, place in small bowl. Add 2 tbsp. (30 mL) water. Cover with plastic wrap and microwave on high (100%) for 1$^1/_2$ minutes.

Nutrition Information

1 serving with 4 tsp. (20 mL) sauce: 159 Calories; 24 g Protein; 3.8 g Total Fat (0.5 g Sat., 36 mg Cholesterol); 77 mg Sodium

Crusty Fish With Tangy Sauce

The cooking time depends on the thickness of the fillets. Serves 4.

TANGY SAUCE		
Canned apricots, drained	14 oz.	398 mL
Dijon mustard	2 tsp.	10 mL
Brown sugar, packed	2 tbsp.	30 mL
Lime juice, fresh or bottled	2 tbsp.	30 mL
Salt	$^1/_8$ tsp.	0.5 mL
Dried crushed chilies	$^1/_8$ tsp.	0.5 mL
Finely chopped almonds	2 tbsp.	30 mL
Fine coconut	1 tbsp.	15 mL
Salt	$^1/_4$ tsp.	1 mL
Pepper, sprinkle		
Egg white (large), room temperature	1	1
Cod, snapper, roughy or halibut fillets	4 × 5 oz.	4 × 140 g

Tangy Sauce: Measure 6 sauce ingredients into blender or food processor. Process until puréed. Pour into small saucepan. Bring to a boil. Reduce heat and simmer, uncovered, for 3 to 4 minutes. Keep warm. Makes 1 cup (250 mL) sauce. ■ Combine almonds, coconut, salt and pepper in small bowl. In separate bowl, beat egg white until stiff. Fold almond mixture into egg white. ■ Pat surface of each fish fillet with paper towel to make it as dry as possible. Divide egg white mixture evenly on surface of each fillet. Lay fillets on lightly greased baking sheet with sides. Bake on bottom rack in 400°F (205°C) oven for 5 minutes. Move to center rack. Broil for 3 minutes until fish flakes easily and topping is golden and crisp. Drizzle warm sauce over fillets or lay fillets on bed of warm sauce.

Nutrition Information

1 serving with $^1/_4$ cup (60 mL) sauce: 210 Calories; 28 g Protein; 4.3 g Total Fat (1.2 g Sat., 60.2 mg Cholesterol); 393 mg Sodium

Fish In Parchment Packets

This takes about 30 minutes to prepare but it's easy and fun to make. Very impressive to serve to company. Serves 4. Pictured on page 89.

New red potatoes, diced into $^1/_2$ inch (12 mm) chunks	2	2
Boiling water, to cover		
Salt (optional)	1 tsp.	5 mL

(continued on next page)

Boneless cod fillets	4 × 5 oz.	4 × 140 g
Lemon pepper	$^{1}/_{2}$ tsp.	2 mL
Salt	1 tsp.	5 mL
Large red onion, diced	1	1
Large red or yellow pepper, diced	1	1
Medium tomatoes, seeded and diced into 1 inch (2.5 cm) chunks	2	2
Chopped fresh oregano	$2^{1}/_{2}$ tbsp.	37 mL
Olive oil (or use cooking spray)	1 tsp.	5 mL
Crumbled feta cheese (optional)	$^{1}/_{4}$ cup	60 mL

Boil potato in water and salt for 2 minutes. Drain and cool slightly. ■ Fold 4 pieces of parchment paper (10 × 13 inches, 25 × 32 cm each) in half, lengthwise. Open. Place 1 cod fillet on bottom half of each piece of parchment paper leaving 1 inch (2.5 cm) border along bottom and sides. Season fillets with lemon pepper and salt. Place about $^{1}/_{4}$ amount of potato, onion, pepper and tomato on top of each fillet. Sprinkle each with about 2 tsp. (10 mL) oregano. Lightly oil surface of vegetables. Fold top half of parchment paper over fish and vegetables meeting bottom edge. Fold bottom edge over several times to crease and seal. Fold and twist side edges together in crescent shape around fish and vegetables. ■ Place packets on 2 large ungreased baking sheets. Bake in 450°F (230°C) oven for 13 to 15 minutes until puffed and golden brown. With scissors, cut an "X" in top and fold points back. ■ Garnish with feta cheese.

Nutrition Information

1 serving: 215 Calories; 27 g Protein; 2.5 g Total Fat (0.4 g Sat., 60.2 mg Cholesterol); 764 mg Sodium

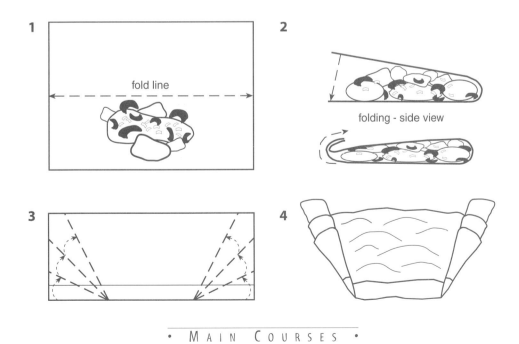

1

fold line

2

folding - side view

3

4

New Age Meatloaf

Meatloaf that is in step with the times! Low in fat and quick to prepare. Serves 8.

Extra lean ground beef	³/₄ **lb.**	**340 g**
Lean ground chicken or turkey	³/₄ **lb.**	**340 g**
Fine dry bread crumbs	¹/₂ **cup**	**125 mL**
Egg white (large)	**1**	**1**
Medium carrot, cut into 1 inch (2.5 cm) chunks	**1**	**1**
Small onion, cut into chunks	**1**	**1**
Ketchup	¹/₄ **cup**	**60 mL**
Garlic clove	**1**	**1**
Worcestershire sauce	**1 tsp.**	**5 mL**
Celery seed	¹/₄ **tsp.**	**1 mL**
Salt	**1 tsp.**	**5 mL**
Pepper	¹/₈ **tsp.**	**0.5 mL**

Combine ground beef, chicken and bread crumbs in large bowl. ■ Put remaining 9 ingredients into blender. Process until carrot is very finely chopped. Add meat mixture. Mix very well. Form into loaf shape about 4 × 10 inches (10 × 25 cm). Place in lightly greased 9 × 13 inch (22 × 33 cm) baking dish. Cover with foil. Bake in 350°F (175°C) oven for 1 hour. Remove foil. Bake for 15 to 30 minutes until no pink remains in center of loaf.

Nutrition Information

1 serving: 196 Calories; 21 g Protein; 7.7 g Total Fat (2.8 Sat., 56.7 mg Cholesterol); 579 mg Sodium

Garlic Flank Steak Roll

This looks so attractive served sliced on a platter over a bed of rice. Serves 6.

Flank steak, trimmed of fat	**1¹/₂ lbs.**	**680 g**
Small onion, chopped	**1**	**1**
Garlic cloves, minced	**4**	**4**
Olive oil	**1 tsp.**	**5 mL**
Fresh thyme leaves	**1 tbsp.**	**15 mL**
Chopped fresh basil	¹/₄ **cup**	**60 mL**
Chopped fresh parsley	¹/₄ **cup**	**60 mL**
Paprika	¹/₂ **tsp.**	**2 mL**
Salt	¹/₄ **tsp.**	**1 mL**
Freshly ground pepper	¹/₄ **tsp.**	**1 mL**
Water	**2 tbsp.**	**30 mL**

(continued on next page)

Pound flank steak with meat mallet or rolling pin until $^3/_8$ inch (8 mm) thick. ■ Sauté onion and garlic in oil in non-stick skillet until golden and very soft. Put mixture into blender or food processor. Add thyme, basil, parsley, paprika, salt, pepper and water. Process until pasty with small chunks of onion. Spread over surface of flank steak. Roll tightly, with grain of steak. Tie butchers' string at 2 inch (5 cm) intervals along roll.

Barbecue Method: Barbecue over medium, indirect heat for 1 hour.

Oven Method: Broil rolls in oven on rack 4 inches (10 cm) away from heat. Turn frequently to brown all sides. Transfer to small roaster. Roast, covered, in 300°F (150°C) oven for 30 minutes.

Nutrition Information

1 serving: 201 Calories; 25 g Protein; 9.2 g Total Fat (3.7 g Sat., 46.1 mg Cholesterol); 186 mg Sodium

Cranberry Pork Tenderloin

An elegant but simple presentation. Only minutes to prepare. Serves 6.

Pork tenderloin	1$^1/_2$ lbs.	680 g
Whole cranberry sauce	14 oz.	398 mL
Onion powder	$^1/_2$ tsp.	2 mL
Grated orange zest	$^1/_2$ tsp.	2 mL
Ground nutmeg, just a pinch		

"Butterfly" tenderloin by cutting horizontally from one long side to almost through other side. Open out to lay flat. Lay on lightly greased baking sheet with sides. ■ Combine remaining 4 ingredients in small bowl. Mix well. Spoon over opened surface of pork. Bake, uncovered, in 400°F (205°C) oven for 30 minutes until pork is no longer pink.

Nutrition Information

1 serving: 245 Calories; 24 g Protein; 2.9 g Total Fat (1 g Sat., 63.9 mg Cholesterol); 78 mg Sodium

Vegetable Layered Polenta

It's polenta instead of pasta in this lasagne-type dish. Serves 8. Pictured on page 36.

Water	6 cups	1.5 L
Salt	1$\frac{1}{2}$ tsp.	7 mL
Cornmeal	1$\frac{1}{2}$ cups	375 mL
Olive oil	$\frac{1}{2}$ tsp.	2 mL
Chopped onion	1 cup	250 mL
Garlic cloves, crushed	2	2
Sliced fresh mushrooms	2 cups	500 mL
Zucchini slices, with peel, quartered lengthwise and sliced $\frac{1}{2}$ inch (12 mm) thick	3 cups	750 mL
Canned stewed tomatoes, with juice, chopped	28 oz.	796 mL
Chopped fresh sweet basil	$\frac{1}{4}$ cup	60 mL
Granulated sugar	1 tsp.	5 mL
Hot pepper sauce	$\frac{1}{8}$ tsp.	0.5 mL
1% mozzarella process cheese slices	6	6
Grated part-skim mozzarella cheese	$\frac{1}{2}$ cup	125 mL
Grated fresh Parmesan cheese	1 tbsp.	15 mL

Bring water and salt to a boil in large saucepan. Reduce heat. Slowly add cornmeal, stirring constantly with whisk for about 20 minutes until mixture is very thick and leaves sides of saucepan. Lightly grease a piece of waxed paper, 25 inches (62 cm) long. Spread polenta out to an 8 x 24 inch (20 x 60 cm) rectangle. Set aside to cool and set. ■ Heat olive oil in large non-stick skillet. Sauté onion, garlic and mushrooms for 5 minutes. Stir in zucchini. Sauté for 5 minutes until zucchini starts to soften. Add tomatoes, basil, sugar and pepper sauce. Bring to a rolling boil. Simmer, uncovered, for 10 minutes until thickened and slightly reduced. Cut cooled polenta in half crosswise.
■ To assemble, layer as follows in greased 8 x 12 inch (20 x 30 cm) baking dish:

1. $\frac{1}{2}$ vegetable sauce.
2. $\frac{1}{2}$ polenta.
3. All mozzarella cheese slices.
4. Remaining $\frac{1}{2}$ vegetable sauce.
5. Remaining $\frac{1}{2}$ polenta.
6. All of grated mozzarella cheese.
7. All of Parmesan cheese.

Bake in 350°F (175°C) oven for 15 minutes until hot and cheese is melted.

N u t r i t i o n   I n f o r m a t i o n

1 serving: 202 Calories; 11 g Protein; 2.8 g Total Fat (1.1 g Sat., 8.1 mg Cholesterol); 1041 mg Sodium

Muffins & Coffee Cakes

uffins and coffee cakes are perfect to serve at a brunch gathering or coffee party. Why bother with high-fat products when you have such a great selection of low-fat recipes at your fingertips? Each of these recipes uses the minimum amount of fat necessary to maintain a moist texture and delicious taste.

Peach Nut Muffins

A small amount of nuts add such a nice flavor. Dried peach in every bite. Makes 12 muffins. Pictured on page 107.

All-purpose flour	1$^1/_4$ **cups**	300 mL
Whole wheat flour	**1 cup**	250 mL
Brown sugar, packed	$^2/_3$ **cup**	150 mL
Baking powder	**1 tbsp.**	15 mL
Salt	$^1/_4$ **tsp.**	1 mL
Canned peaches, with juice, puréed in blender	**14 oz.**	398 mL
Egg white (large), fork-beaten	**1**	1
Vanilla	$^1/_2$ **tsp.**	2 mL
Chopped dried peaches	$^1/_2$ **cup**	125 mL
Large egg	**1**	1
Canola oil	**2 tbsp.**	30 mL
Finely chopped pecans	**1 tbsp.**	15 mL
Flaked coconut	**1 tbsp.**	15 mL

Combine first 5 ingredients in large bowl. Make a well in center. ■ Combine next 6 ingredients in medium bowl. Pour into well of dry ingredients. Stir just until moistened. Divide among 12 lightly greased muffin cups. ■ Combine pecans and coconut in small cup. Sprinkle over each muffin. Bake in 350°F (175°C) oven for 20 minutes until wooden pick inserted in muffin comes out clean. Let stand for 5 minutes. Remove muffins to wire rack to cool.

Nutrition Information

1 muffin: 204 Calories; 4 g Protein; 3.8 g Total Fat (0.7 g Sat., 18 mg Cholesterol); 77 mg Sodium

Apple Bran Muffins

The applesauce and buttermilk give these muffins moisture without the high fat. Makes 12 muffins. Pictured on page 107.

All-purpose flour	**1 cup**	**250 mL**
Whole wheat flour	**1 cup**	**250 mL**
Natural bran	**1 cup**	**250 mL**
Brown sugar, packed	**¹/₃ cup**	**75 mL**
Baking powder	**1 tbsp.**	**15 mL**
Salt	**¹/₂ tsp.**	**2 mL**
Applesauce	**1 cup**	**250 mL**
Canola oil	**2 tbsp.**	**30 mL**
Large egg	**1**	**1**
1% buttermilk	**¹/₂ cup**	**125 mL**
Vanilla	**1 tsp.**	**5 mL**
Maple flavoring	**¹/₂ tsp.**	**2 mL**
Finely chopped dates	**¹/₄ cup**	**60 mL**

Stir first 6 ingredients together in large bowl. Make a well in center. ■ Whisk applesauce, oil, egg, buttermilk, vanilla and maple flavoring together in small bowl. Stir in dates. Pour into well of dry ingredients. Stir just until moistened. Divide among 12 lightly greased muffin cups. Bake in 375°F (190°C) oven for 20 minutes until wooden pick inserted in muffin comes out clean. Let stand for 5 minutes. Remove muffins to wire rack to cool.

Nutrition Information

1 muffin: 163 Calories; 4 g Protein; 3.4 g Total Fat (0.4 g Sat., 18.3 mg Cholesterol); 137 mg Sodium

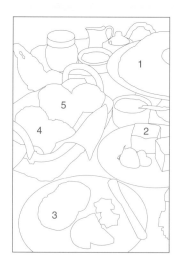

1. Orange Coffee Cake, page 111
2. Breakfast Cornmeal Cake, page 109
3. Orange Oatmeal Muffins, page 110
4. Apple Bran Muffins, page 106
5. Peach Nut Muffins, page 105

Breakfast Cornmeal Cake

Try using a mixture of colors and flavors of jam. Cuts into 12 pieces. Pictured on page 107.

Cornmeal	**1¹/₂ cups**	**375 mL**
All-purpose flour	**1¹/₂ cups**	**375 mL**
Granulated sugar	**²/₃ cup**	**150 mL**
Baking powder	**4 tsp.**	**20 mL**
Baking soda	**¹/₂ tsp.**	**2 mL**
Salt	**¹/₂ tsp.**	**2 mL**
Large egg, fork-beaten	**1**	**1**
Egg white (large), fork-beaten	**1**	**1**
1% buttermilk	**1¹/₂ cups**	**375 mL**
Hard margarine, melted	**¹/₄ cup**	**60 mL**
Thick raspberry jam, or your favorite	**¹/₄ cup**	**60 mL**

Combine first 6 ingredients in medium bowl. Make a well in center. ■ Combine egg and egg white in small bowl. Add buttermilk and margarine. Pour mixture into well of dry ingredients. Stir just until flour is moistened. Spread batter evenly in lightly greased 9 × 13 inch (22 × 33 cm) pan. ■ Spoon jam, in 3 rows of 4, on top of cornmeal batter, using 1 tsp. (5 mL) per spoonful. Push jam slightly into batter. Bake in 375°F (190°C) oven for 35 minutes until wooden pick inserted in center comes out clean.

Nutrition Information

1 piece: 247 Calories; 5 g Protein; 4.9 g Total Fat (1.2 g Sat., 19.1 mg Cholesterol); 265 mg Sodium

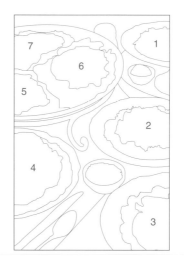

1. Linguini With Clam Sauce, page 112
2. Chick Pea And Tomato Pasta, page 114
3. Creamy Dijon Spinach Sauce, page 134
4. Angel Chicken, page 115
5. Shiitake Wine Sauce, page 135
6. Black Bean Vegetable Sauce, Page 134
7. Roasted Pepper Sauce, page 133

Orange Oatmeal Muffins

The whole wheat flour makes this a more nutritious and heavier muffin. Best served warm. Makes 12 muffins. Pictured on page 107.

Quick-cooking rolled oats (not instant)	**1 cup**	**250 mL**
Whole wheat flour	**1¹/₂ cups**	**375 mL**
Granulated sugar	**¹/₃ cup**	**75 mL**
Baking powder	**1 tsp.**	**5 mL**
Baking soda	**1 tsp.**	**5 mL**
Salt	**¹/₄ tsp.**	**1 mL**
Grated orange peel	**2 tsp.**	**10 mL**
1% buttermilk	**1 cup**	**250 mL**
Canola oil	**2 tbsp.**	**30 mL**
Large egg, fork-beaten	**1**	**1**
TOPPING		
Quick-cooking rolled oats (not instant)	**1 tbsp.**	**15 mL**
Granulated sugar	**1 tbsp.**	**15 mL**
Grated orange peel	**¹/₂ tsp.**	**2 mL**

Combine first 7 ingredients in large bowl. Stir. Make a well in center. ■ Combine buttermilk, oil and egg in small bowl. Pour into well of dry ingredients. Stir just until moistened. Divide among 12 lightly greased muffin cups. ■ **Topping:** Combine all 3 ingredients. Sprinkle over each muffin. Bake in 350°F (175°C) oven for 15 minutes until wooden pick inserted in muffin comes out clean. Let stand for 5 minutes. Remove muffins to wire rack to cool.

N u t r i t i o n   I n f o r m a t i o n

1 muffin: 145 Calories; 5 g Protein; 3.7 g Total Fat (0.6 g Sat., 18.7 mg Cholesterol); 201 mg Sodium

Be careful not to overbake low-fat baked products. Lower the oven temperature by 25°F (4°C) to help prevent food from drying out. Check for doneness a bit sooner than indicated in the recipe.

Orange Coffee Cake

The ricotta cheese adds moisture to this coffee cake. Ricotta means "re-cooked" and gets its name from the fact that the cheese is made by heating the whey from another cooked cheese. This is a golden brown braided wreath. Cuts into 16 pieces. Pictured on page 107.

All-purpose flour	2 cups	500 mL
Envelope instant yeast (1 level tbsp., 15 mL)	1 x $^1/_4$ oz.	1 × 8 g
Freshly squeezed or prepared orange juice	$^3/_4$ cup	175 mL
Skim milk	$^3/_4$ cup	175 mL
Granulated sugar	$^1/_2$ cup	125 mL
Large egg, fork-beaten	1	1
Part-skim ricotta cheese	$^1/_2$ cup	125 mL
Grated orange peel	1 tbsp.	15 mL
All-purpose flour	2 cups	500 mL
Canola oil (or use cooking spray)	$^1/_2$ tsp.	2 mL
ORANGE GLAZE		
Icing (confectioner's) sugar	1 cup	250 mL
Freshly squeezed or prepared orange juice	2 tbsp.	30 mL

Combine first amount of flour and yeast in medium bowl. ■ Stir orange juice, skim milk and sugar together in small saucepan. Heat until sugar is dissolved. Pour into large bowl. Add flour mixture. Whisk until smooth. ■ Stir egg, ricotta cheese and orange peel together in small bowl. Add to orange juice mixture. Mix well. ■ Gradually add second amount of flour until dough can be kneaded. Knead for 5 to 10 minutes on floured surface, adding more flour, if necessary, to prevent sticking. Put into large bowl. Oil surface of dough. (Cooking spray works best.) Cover with clean damp tea towel. Let rise in warm place for 45 minutes until double in size. Punch dough down. Divide into 3 equal parts. Roll each into 18 to 20 inch (45 to 50 cm) long rope. Braid 3 ropes together. Make wreath on lightly greased baking sheet. Pinch ends together. Cover with tea towel. Let rise for 30 minutes until doubled in size. Bake in 375°F (190°C) oven for 25 minutes. Cover top with foil if becoming too brown. Remove from pan to wire rack to cool. ■ **Orange Glaze:** Combine icing sugar and orange juice in small bowl. Stir well. Drizzle over warm coffee cake.

Nutrition Information

1 piece: 205 Calories; 5 g Protein; 1.5 g Total Fat (0.6 g Sat., 16.2 mg Cholesterol); 22 mg Sodium

Pasta

asta most often consists of durum wheat flour and a liquid such as water or milk. Some doughs also have egg added and will therefore have a higher fat content. Dough made with only flour and eggs is usually referred to as noodles. While pasta is naturally low in fat, the same thing can't always be said about the sauce. Relax and enjoy these satisfying recipes, knowing that you have created a delicious, low-fat meal everyone can enjoy. Add a salad and bun and your meal is complete!

Linguini With Clam Sauce

To rewarm leftovers just add a bit of water or milk before heating. Serves 8 to 10. Pictured on page 108.

CLAM SAUCE		
Olive oil	2 tsp.	10 mL
Garlic cloves, minced	2	2
Green onions, sliced	4	4
Sliced fresh mushrooms	2 cups	500 mL
Canned baby clams, drained, liquid and clams reserved	2 × 5 oz.	2 × 142 g
White wine	1/2 cup	125 mL
Dried sweet basil	2 tsp.	10 mL
Dried parsley flakes	1 tbsp.	15 mL
Non-fat spreadable cream cheese	8 oz.	225 g
Reserved clams		
Linguini pasta, uncooked	10 oz.	300 g
Grated fresh Parmesan cheese (optional)		

Clam Sauce: Heat oil in large non-stick wok or skillet. Sauté garlic, green onion and mushrooms until soft. Add liquid from clams, white wine, basil and parsley. Cover. Simmer for 5 minutes. ■ Add cream cheese, stirring constantly. Add clams. Keep sauce warm. ■ Cook linguini according to package directions. Drain. Toss with warm sauce. ■ Sprinkle with Parmesan cheese if desired. Serve immediately.

Nutrition Information

1/8 recipe: 247 Calories; 16 g Protein; 2.6 g Total Fat (0.3 g Sat., 23.8 mg Cholesterol); 45 mg Sodium

Stuffed Turkey Scallopini

What a wonderful stuffing surprise inside! There is quite a difference in flavor (and cost) between the prosciutto and the ham. Pick your preference. Serves 8.

Lean prosciutto or cooked ham, chopped	**4 oz.**	**113 g**
Grated part-skim mozzarella cheese	**1/2 cup**	**125 g**
Garlic clove, minced	**1**	**1**
Chopped fresh parsley	**1 tbsp.**	**15 mL**
Chopped fresh basil	**1 tbsp.**	**15 mL**
Thin turkey scallopini	**1 lb.**	**454 g**
Canned Italian plum tomatoes, with juice	**28 oz.**	**796 mL**
Granulated sugar	**1 tsp.**	**5 mL**
Dried sweet basil	**1 tsp.**	**5 mL**
Dried oregano	**1/2 tsp.**	**2 mL**
Pepper	**1/4 tsp.**	**1 mL**
Cornstarch	**1 tbsp.**	**15 mL**
Water	**1 tbsp.**	**15 mL**
Spaghetti pasta	**8 oz.**	**225 g**
Boiling water	**8 cups**	**2 L**
Salt (optional)	**1 tsp.**	**5 mL**

Combine prosciutto, cheese, garlic, parsley and basil in small bowl. ■ Pound out scallopini with flat side of mallet until 1/4 inch (6 mm) thick. Divide into 8 serving size pieces. Place about 3 tbsp. (50 mL) prosciutto mixture on narrow end of each scallopini. Roll up, tucking in sides. Hold closed with wooden picks or tie with butchers' string. Lightly grease large non-stick skillet. Brown rolls on all sides until golden. ■ Chop tomatoes coarsely and add, with juice, to skillet. Add sugar, basil, oregano and pepper. Cover. Simmer for 30 minutes. Remove rolls to plate. Keep warm. ■ Mix cornstarch and water in small cup. Stir into tomato sauce to thicken slightly. Makes 3 cups (750 mL) sauce. ■ Cook pasta in boiling water and salt in large Dutch oven for 7 to 9 minutes until tender but firm. Drain. Rinse. Drain again. Arrange in large pasta bowl. Pour sauce over pasta and toss lightly. Serve with turkey rolls.

Nutrition Information

1 serving: 259 Calories; 24 g Protein; 5.6 g Total Fat (2.5 g Sat., 52.9 mg Cholesterol); 484 mg Sodium

Fresh Tomato Pasta

Radiatore pasta is Italian for "little radiators." Its small chunky shape resembles tiny radiators with rippled edges. Makes 9 cups (2.25 L).

Olive oil	2 tsp.	10 mL
Garlic cloves, crushed	3	3
Large onion, finely chopped	1	1
Large plum tomatoes, finely chopped	6	6
Radiatore pasta	5 cups	1.25 L
Tomato sauce	7¹/₂ oz.	213 mL
Chopped fresh sweet basil	¹/₄ cup	60 mL
Granulated sugar	1 tbsp.	15 mL
Grated fresh Parmesan cheese (optional)		

Heat oil on medium in large saucepan. Sauté garlic and onion for 4 minutes. ■ Add tomatoes. Sauté for 8 minutes until onion and tomato are soft. ■ Cook pasta according to package directions. Drain. ■ Add tomato sauce, basil and sugar to onion mixture. Stir. Simmer, uncovered, until hot. Toss sauce and pasta together. ■ Sprinkle with Parmesan cheese if desired.

Nutrition Information

1¹/₂ cups (375 mL): 316 Calories; 10 g Protein; 3.1 g Total Fat (0.4 g Sat., 0 mg Cholesterol); 239 mg Sodium

Chick Pea And Tomato Pasta

Only 15 minutes preparation time. Adding the liquid with the chick peas enhances the flavor but increases the sodium considerably. To reduce the sodium, omit the liquid and add ¹/₃ cup (75 mL) water. Serves 4 to 6. Pictured on page 108.

Olive oil	1 tbsp.	15 mL
Garlic cloves, minced	2	2
Small onion, slivered lengthwise	1	1
Canned diced tomatoes, with juice	28 oz.	796 mL
Finely chopped fresh parsley	¹/₄ cup	60 mL
Dried sweet basil	1 tsp.	5 mL
Dried oregano	³/₄ tsp.	4 mL
Granulated sugar	¹/₂ tsp.	2 mL
Freshly ground pepper	¹/₄ tsp.	1 mL
Canned chick peas (garbanzo beans), with liquid	19 oz.	540 mL
Rotini, radiatore or bow pasta	10 oz.	280 mL
Freshly grated Parmesan cheese	2 tbsp.	30 mL

(continued on next page)

Heat oil in large non-stick skillet. Sauté garlic and onion until onion is slightly soft. Stir in tomatoes, parsley, basil, oregano, sugar and pepper. Bring to a boil. Simmer, uncovered, for 15 minutes. ■ Stir in chick peas. Simmer for 10 minutes until thickened. ■ Cook pasta according to package directions. Drain. Combine pasta with sauce in large serving bowl. Sprinkle with Parmesan cheese.

Nutrition Information

1/4 recipe: 542 Calories; 20 g Protein; 7.5 g Total Fat (1.4 g Sat., 2 mg Cholesterol); 794 mg Sodium

Angel Chicken

Cook the pasta during the second baking time of the vegetables. Serves 4. Pictured on page 108.

Canned stewed tomatoes, chopped	14 oz.	398 mL
Garlic clove, crushed	1	1
Diced zucchini	2 cups	500 mL
Yellow pepper, diced	1	1
Dried sweet basil	2 tsp.	10 mL
Granulated sugar	1/4 tsp.	1 mL
Boneless, skinless chicken breast halves	4	4
Grated part-skim mozzarella cheese	1 cup	250 mL
Angel hair or cappellini pasta	8 oz.	225 g
Boiling water	8 cups	2 L
Salt (optional)	1 tsp.	5 mL
Grated fresh Parmesan cheese	1 tbsp.	15 mL

Mix tomatoes with garlic in small bowl. Pour into ungreased 2 quart (2 L) casserole dish. Layer zucchini, yellow pepper, basil and sugar over tomato mixture. Lay chicken over vegetable mixture. Spoon a bit of tomato mixture in bottom of dish, over chicken. Bake, uncovered, in 350°F (175°C) oven for 1 hour. Sprinkle with cheese. Bake, uncovered, for about 10 minutes, until cheese is melted. Carefully remove chicken and place in bowl. Set aside. ■ Cook pasta in boiling water and salt in large uncovered Dutch oven for 7 to 9 minutes until tender but firm. Drain. Rinse. Drain again. Place on large serving platter. Pour tomato-vegetable mixture over pasta and toss lightly to combine. Lay chicken over pasta. ■ Sprinkle with Parmesan cheese just before serving.

Nutrition Information

1 serving: 468 Calories; 44 g Protein; 7.9 g Total Fat (3.9 g Sat., 87.1 mg Cholesterol); 522 mg Sodium

Veggie Lasagne

This vegetable lasagne can be prepared in 45 minutes. Cuts into 8 to 10 pieces.

Lasagne noodles	**9**	**9**
Canned crushed tomatoes	**14 oz.**	**398 mL**
Canned diced tomatoes, with juice	**14 oz.**	**398 mL**
Medium onion, finely chopped	**1**	**1**
Sliced fresh mushrooms	**2 cups**	**500 mL**
Garlic cloves, minced	**2**	**2**
Dried oregano	**1 tsp.**	**5 mL**
Granulated sugar	**1/2 tsp.**	**2 mL**
Chopped fresh parsley	**1/4 cup**	**60 mL**
Part-skim ricotta cheese	**1 lb.**	**475 g**
Grated carrot	**3/4 cup**	**175 mL**
Chopped fresh parsley	**1/4 cup**	**60 mL**
Coarsely chopped cooked broccoli	**4 cups**	**1 L**
Freshly grated Parmesan cheese	**2 tbsp.**	**30 mL**
Egg white (large), fork-beaten	**1**	**1**
Salt	**1 tsp.**	**5 mL**
Pepper	**1/4 tsp.**	**1 mL**
Grated part-skim mozzarella cheese	**1 cup**	**250 mL**
Grated fresh Parmesan cheese	**2 tbsp.**	**30 mL**

Cook noodles according to package directions. Drain. Cool in cold water until ready to use. ■ Combine next 8 ingredients in medium saucepan. Bring to a boil. Reduce heat. Cover. Simmer for 10 minutes. Remove from heat.■ Combine next 8 ingredients in medium bowl. Assemble lasagne in lightly greased 9 x 13 inch (22 x 33 cm) pan as follows:

1. 1/4 tomato sauce.
2. 3 lasagne noodles.
3. 1/2 cheese mixture.
4. 1/4 tomato sauce.
5. 3 lasagne noodles.
6. 1/2 cheese mixture.
7. 1/4 tomato sauce.
8. 3 lasagne noodles.
9. 1/4 tomato sauce.

Cover with foil that has been lightly greased. Bake in 350°F (175°C) oven for 1 hour. Remove foil. ■ Sprinkle with mozzarella cheese and second amount of Parmesan cheese. Bake, uncovered, for 15 minutes until cheese is melted. Let stand for 15 minutes before cutting.

Nutrition Information

1/8 recipe: 280 Calories; 19 g Protein; 8.9 g Total Fat (5.1 g Sat., 29.1 mg Cholesterol); 733 mg Sodium

Pasta With Lemon Vegetables

Use any combination of vegetables to make this speedy pasta dish. Have the vegetables steaming as the pasta cooks. Serves 8.

Skim evaporated milk	**1 cup**	**250 mL**
Non-fat spreadable cream cheese	**8 oz.**	**225 g**
Cornstarch	**2 tbsp.**	**30 mL**
White wine	**2 tbsp.**	**30 mL**
Rotini, radiatore or bow pasta	**3 cups**	**750 mL**
Boiling water	**2¹/₂ qts.**	**2.5 L**
Salt (optional)	**2 tsp.**	**10 mL**
Low-fat chicken bouillon cube	**¹/₄ × ¹/₃ oz.**	**¹/₄ × 10.5 g**
Boiling water	**¹/₄ cup**	**60 mL**
Fresh lemon juice	**2 tbsp.**	**30 mL**
Broccoli florets	**1 cup**	**250 mL**
Sliced asparagus, cut diagonally in 1 inch (2.5 cm) lengths	**1 cup**	**250 mL**
Fresh pea pods	**1 cup**	**250 mL**
Sliced fresh green beans, cut diagonally into 1¹/₂ inch (3.8 cm) lengths	**1 cup**	**250 mL**
Grated lemon zest	**1 tbsp.**	**15 mL**
Grated fresh Parmesan cheese (optional)	**2 tbsp.**	**30 mL**
Freshly ground pepper, sprinkle		

Heat evaporated milk in medium saucepan. Add cream cheese and stir until melted. Stir cornstarch and wine together in small cup. Add to cream cheese mixture. Stir until bubbling and thickened. ■ Cook pasta in boiling water and salt in large uncovered Dutch oven for 8 to 10 minutes until tender but firm. Drain. Rinse. Drain again. Put back into Dutch oven and keep warm. ■ Dissolve partial bouillon cube in boiling water in small cup. Pour into large non-stick skillet or wok. Add lemon juice. Heat to boiling. ■ Add broccoli, asparagus, pea pods and green beans. Simmer, covered, for 6 minutes, stirring once at half time. Sprinkle lemon zest over top. ■ Combine pasta, vegetables and sauce. Sprinkle with Parmesan cheese and pepper.

Nutrition Information

1 serving: 207 Calories; 10 g Protein; 0.8 g Total Fat (0.2 g Sat., 1.2 mg Cholesterol); 108 mg Sodium

Salads

S alads are a delicious part of any light and healthy diet, but be wary of the type of dressings you choose as they can often be very high in fat. Here are some unique salad recipes that include a zesty collection of incredible dressings. Take a moment to explore the ins and outs of making low-fat dressings by following these fast, easy recipes.

Tabbouleh

Bulgur consists of wheat kernels that have been steamed, dried and crushed. Serve cold with a slice of bread. Makes 4^1/$_2$ cups (1.1 L). Pictured on page 144.

Bulgur	**1 cup**	**250 mL**
Boiling water	**1 cup**	**250 mL**
Plum tomatoes, diced	**2**	**2**
Thinly sliced red onion	**^{1}/$_2$ cup**	**125 mL**
Yellow or green pepper, seeded and diced	**^{1}/$_2$**	**^{1}/$_2$**
Thinly sliced green onion	**^{1}/$_4$ cup**	**60 mL**
Chopped fresh mint	**^{1}/$_3$ cup**	**75 mL**
Chopped fresh parsley	**^{1}/$_2$ cup**	**125 mL**
LEMON DRESSING		
Lemon juice, fresh or bottled	**^{1}/$_4$ cup**	**60 mL**
Garlic clove, minced	**1**	**1**
Lemon pepper	**^{1}/$_2$ tsp.**	**2 mL**
Olive oil	**1 tbsp.**	**15 mL**
Apple juice	**^{1}/$_4$ cup**	**60 mL**
Salt	**^{1}/$_4$ tsp.**	**1 mL**

Place bulgur in bowl and pour boiling water over. Stir. Let stand for ^{1}/$_2$ hour until water is absorbed. ■ Add next 6 ingredients . Mix well. ■ **Lemon Dressing:** Combine all 6 ingredients in small bowl. Stir. Pour over bulgur mixture. Cover. Refrigerate for at least 2 hours.

Nutrition Information

^{3}/$_4$ cup (175 mL): 132 Calories; 4 g Protein; 2.8 g Total Fat (0.4 g Sat., 0 mg Cholesterol); 125 mg Sodium

Variation: For tangy flavor, add 2 tsp. (10 mL) balsamic vinegar.

Tangy Broccoli Salad

A combination of broccoli florets and stems works just as well. Makes 6 cups (1.5 L).
Pictured on page 36.

Yogurt Cheese, page 67	**¹/₂ cup**	**125 mL**
Non-fat sour cream	**¹/₄ cup**	**60 mL**
Granulated sugar	**1 tbsp.**	**15 mL**
Salt	**¹/₄ tsp.**	**1 mL**
White vinegar	**1 tbsp.**	**15 mL**
Broccoli florets	**4 cups**	**1 L**
Golden raisins	**¹/₂ cup**	**125 mL**
Medium red onion, very thinly sliced	**¹/₂**	**¹/₂**
Roasted and salted sunflower seeds	**2 tbsp.**	**30 mL**
Bacon slices, cooked crisp and crumbled	**2**	**2**

Mix first 5 ingredients in small bowl. ■ Combine remaining 5 ingredients in large bowl. Pour yogurt cheese mixture over. Refrigerate for at least 1 hour.

Nutrition Information

1 cup (250 mL): 120 Calories; 6 g Protein; 2.7 g Total Fat (0.6 g Sat., 2.6 mg Cholesterol); 222 mg Sodium

Raspberry Dressing

Drizzle over green salad or fresh fruit. Makes 1 cup (250 mL).

Frozen unsweetened raspberries, thawed	**1 cup**	**250 mL**
White wine vinegar	**4 tsp.**	**20 mL**
Granulated sugar	**3 tsp.**	**15 mL**

Put raspberries into blender. Process until smooth. ■ Add vinegar and sugar. Process.

Nutrition Information

2 tbsp. (30 mL): 14 Calories; trace Protein; 0.1 g Total Fat (0 g Sat., 0 mg Cholesterol); trace Sodium

....

Don't be fooled by the "light" label on oils. They are usually lighter in color, not lower in calories or fat.

Antipasto Salad

Serve as the first course or as a main course accompaniment. Great with any barbecue meal.
Makes 10 cups (2.5 L). Pictured on page 90.

ITALIAN DRESSING

Condensed chicken broth (10 oz., 284 mL)	**1 cup**	**250 mL**
Cornstarch	**2 tsp.**	**10 mL**
White wine vinegar	**³/₄ cup**	**175 mL**
Dried sweet basil	**2 tsp.**	**10 mL**
Dried oregano	**2 tsp.**	**10 mL**
Garlic cloves, crushed	**2**	**2**
Granulated sugar	**1 tsp.**	**5 mL**
Broccoli florets	**2 cups**	**500 mL**
Small red onion, thinly sliced	**1**	**1**
Medium green pepper, cut into **¹/₄ inch (6 mm) slices**	**1**	**1**
Medium red pepper, cut into **¹/₄ inch (6 mm) slices**	**1**	**1**
Medium yellow pepper, cut into **¹/₄ inch (6 mm) slices**	**1**	**1**
Canned artichoke hearts, drained and **quartered**	**14 oz.**	**398 mL**
Canned chick peas (garbanzo beans), drained	**19 oz.**	**540 mL**
Canned solid white tuna, packed in water, **drained and flaked**	**6¹/₂ oz.**	**184 g**

Italian Dressing: Combine first 7 ingredients in medium saucepan. Bring to a boil, stirring until slightly thickened. Stir in broccoli florets. Remove from heat. Cool to room temperature. ■ Combine remaining 7 ingredients in large bowl. Add dressing. Toss well. Refrigerate for several hours or overnight, stirring occasionally. Before serving, stir salad and drain off dressing.

Nutrition Information

1 cup (250 mL): 99 Calories; 8 g Protein; 1.3 g Total Fat (0.2 g Sat., 6.5 mg Cholesterol); 277 mg Sodium

Variation: Substitute any of the vegetables with thinly sliced zucchini, sliced fresh mushrooms, olives or tomatoes.

Spicy Noodle Salad

Serve immediately or let stand, covered, in the refrigerator overnight. Makes 7 cups (1.75 L), enough for 8 servings. Pictured on page 125.

Broken low-fat instant Chinese noodles	1 cup	250 mL
Boiling water	3 cups	750 mL
Finely shredded Chinese cabbage	3 cups	750 mL
Green onions, thinly sliced	4	4
Medium red pepper, finely diced	1	1
Thinly sliced carrot	1 cup	250 mL
Toasted sesame seeds	1 tbsp.	15 mL
Canola oil	1 tsp.	5 mL
Freshly grated gingerroot	2 tsp.	10 mL
Garlic clove, minced	1	1
Water	$^1/_2$ cup	125 mL
Chicken bouillon powder	1 tsp.	5 mL
Dried crushed chilies	$^1/_4$ tsp.	1 mL
Liquid honey	2 tbsp.	30 mL
Low-sodium soy sauce	2 tbsp.	30 mL
Balsamic vinegar	1 tbsp.	15 mL
Cornstarch	2 tsp.	10 mL

Put noodles into large bowl. Pour boiling water over noodles. Let stand for 5 minutes. Drain. Rinse with cold water. Return to bowl. ■ Add next 5 ingredients and toss together. ■ Heat oil in small skillet or saucepan. Sauté gingerroot and garlic for 1 minute. Add water, bouillon powder, chilies and honey. Bring to a boil. ■ Stir soy sauce, vinegar and cornstarch together in small cup until smooth. Pour into chili mixture. Stir until boiling and thickened. Pour over noodle mixture. Toss.

Nutrition Information

1 serving: 80 Calories; 2 g Protein; 1.5 g Total Fat (0.2 g Sat., 0.1 mg Cholesterol); 249 mg Sodium

Choose non-fat or low-fat salad dressings instead of regular salad dressings, or use herbs, lemon juice and spices to add flavor to vegetables.

Oriental Salad

This is even better the next day. Serves 8. Pictured on page 89.

SAKE DRESSING		
Freshly grated gingerroot	$1/2$-1 tsp.	2-5 mL
Rice wine (such as sake)	$1/4$ cup	60 mL
Granulated sugar	1 tbsp.	15 mL
Low-sodium soy sauce	2 tbsp.	30 mL
Toasted sesame seeds (optional)	2 tsp.	10 mL
White wine vinegar	2 tbsp.	30 mL
Garlic clove, minced	1	1
Dried crushed chilies	$1/4$ tsp.	1 mL
Sesame oil	1 tsp.	5 mL
Broken low-fat instant Chinese noodles	$1^1/4$ cups	300 mL
Finely shredded suey choy	3 cups	750 mL
Julienned jicama	1 cup	250 mL
Grated carrot	$1/2$ cup	125 mL
Green onions, sliced	4	4
Bean sprouts	2 cups	500 mL
Small red pepper, diced	1	1
Canned water chestnuts, drained and coarsely chopped	8 oz.	227 mL

Sake Dressing: Combine 9 ingredients in jar. Cover and shake. ■ Toss remaining 8 ingredients together in large bowl. Pour dressing over top. Toss.

Nutrition Information

1 serving: 95 Calories; 3 g Protein; 0.9 g Total Fat (0.1 g Sat., 0 mg Cholesterol); 169 mg Sodium

Jicama And Corn Salad

Jicama (HEE-kah-mah) is often referred to as the Mexican potato. It is sweet and nutty. Great served raw or cooked. Makes 6 cups (1.5 L). Pictured on page 125.

Canned kernel corn, drained	14 oz.	398 mL
Peeled and diced jicama	2 cups	500 mL
Diced red pepper	1 cup	250 mL
Green onions, sliced thinly	3	3
Yogurt Cheese, page 67	$1/2$ cup	125 mL
Freshly squeezed lemon juice	2 tbsp.	30 mL
Grated lemon peel	1 tsp.	5 mL
Liquid honey	1 tbsp.	15 mL
Hot pepper sauce, dash		

(continued on next page)

Combine corn, jicama, red pepper and green onion in large bowl. ■ Stir next
5 ingredients together in separate bowl. Fold into corn mixture.

N u t r i t i o n   I n f o r m a t i o n

1 cup (250 mL): 93 Calories; 3 g Protein; 0.4 g Total Fat (trace Sat., 0.4 mg Cholesterol);
179 mg Sodium

Creamy Cucumber Cups

The cucumber will stay crisp for up to 3 hours if refrigerated. Serves 6. Pictured on the front cover.

Yogurt Cheese, page 67	**$^1/_2$ cup**	**125 mL**
Non-fat sour cream	**1 cup**	**250 mL**
Juice and grated peel of 1 lemon		
Green onions, thinly sliced	**2**	**2**
Granulated sugar	**1 tbsp.**	**15 mL**
Salt	**$^1/_4$ tsp.**	**1 mL**
Chopped fresh mint	**1 tsp.**	**5 mL**
Chopped fresh sweet basil	**1 tsp.**	**5 mL**
English cucumbers, with peel, quartered lengthwise and sliced	**2**	**2**
Butter lettuce leaves	**6**	**6**
Ground toasted walnuts	**2 tbsp.**	**30 mL**
Raisins	**$^1/_4$ cup**	**60 mL**

Combine first 8 ingredients in medium bowl. ■ Add cucumber to sour cream mixture.
Stir. Cover with plastic wrap. Refrigerate for 1 hour. ■ Place cup-like lettuce leaves on
individual plates. Spoon cucumber mixture into lettuce cups. ■ Sprinkle with toasted
walnuts and raisins.

N u t r i t i o n   I n f o r m a t i o n

1 serving: 105 Calories; 5 g Protein; 2 g Total Fat (0.3 g Sat., 0.8 mg Cholesterol);
167 mg Sodium

Reduce the amounts of nuts and seeds whenever possible.

Bruschetta In A Bowl

Day-old bread is used to decrease the absorption of the liquid in the salad and for ease of cubing. Makes 7 cups (1.75 L). Pictured on page 125.

Cubed day-old Italian bread, cut into 1 inch (2.5 cm) cubes	**4 cups**	**1 L**
Balsamic vinegar	**$^1/_3$ cup**	**75 mL**
English cucumber, with peel, quartered lengthwise and sliced	**1**	**1**
Medium red or yellow pepper, seeded and chopped	**1**	**1**
Plum tomatoes, diced	**3**	**3**
Freshly ground pepper	**$^1/_4$ tsp.**	**1 mL**
Finely chopped fresh sweet basil	**$^1/_4$ cup**	**60 mL**
Sliced pitted ripe olives	**$^1/_4$ cup**	**60 mL**
Olive oil	**2 tsp.**	**10 mL**

Spread bread cubes on large ungreased baking sheet with sides. Bake in 350°F (175°C) oven for 5 minutes. Stir. Bake for 10 to 15 minutes until toasted. ■ Combine remaining 8 ingredients in medium bowl. Add bread cubes. Toss.

Nutrition Information

1 cup (250 mL): 109 Calories; 3 g Protein; 2.1 g Total Fat (0.3 g Sat., 0.3 mg Cholesterol); 184 mg Sodium

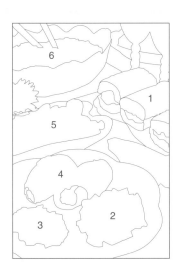

1. Wrapped Salad Loaf, page 81
2. Bruschetta In A Bowl, page 124
3. Jicama And Corn Salad, page 122
4. Spinach-Stuffed Sole, page 98
5. Tomato Pasta Salad, page 131
6. Spicy Noodle Salad, page 121

Jicama Fruit Salad

This makes a large salad. Halve the recipe for a smaller crowd. Makes 16 cups (4 L).

LEMON POPPY SEED DRESSING

Non-fat lemon yogurt	**1 cup**	**250 mL**
Granulated sugar	**1 tsp.**	**5 mL**
Poppy seeds	**1 tsp.**	**5 mL**
Medium butter lettuce heads, torn	**2**	**2**
Medium jicama, cut julienne	**¹/₂**	**¹/₂**
Sliced fresh strawberries	**2 cups**	**500 mL**
Canned mandarin orange segments, drained	**10 oz.**	**284 mL**
Canned pineapple tidbits, drained	**8 oz.**	**227 mL**
Miniature marshmallows	**1 cup**	**250 mL**

Lemon Poppy Seed Dressing: Combine all 3 dressing ingredients in small bowl. Whisk until smooth. ■ Toss remaining 6 ingredients together in large bowl. Spoon onto individual plates. Drizzle dressing over each serving.

Nutrition Information

1 cup (250 mL): 46 Calories; 2 g Protein; 0.3 g Total Fat (trace Sat., 0.5 mg Cholesterol); 17 mg Sodium

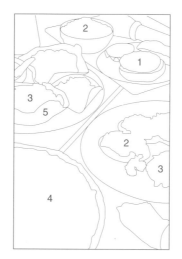

• SALADS •

Mexican Salad

Pinto is Spanish for "painted." The pinto bean has streaks of reddish brown on a pale pink background. If tortilla bowls are not being used, toss the dressing in the bowl with the lettuce mixture. Makes 6 cups (1.5 L) salad, enough to fill 6 to 8 tortilla bowls. Pictured on page 126.

Lean ground beef	**$^1/_2$ lb.**	**225 g**
Taco seasoning mix	**4 tsp.**	**20 mL**
Water	**$^1/_2$ cup**	**125 mL**
Canned pinto beans, drained	**14 oz.**	**398 mL**
Shredded iceberg lettuce	**4 cups**	**1 L**
Small red pepper, diced	**1**	**1**
Very thinly sliced red onion	**1 cup**	**250 mL**
Medium tomato, diced	**1**	**1**
Tortilla Bowls, page 129	**6**	**6**
CHILI DRESSING		
Non-fat yogurt	**$^1/_2$ cup**	**125 mL**
Non-fat sour cream	**$^1/_2$ cup**	**125 mL**
Chili sauce	**3 tbsp.**	**50 mL**
Onion powder	**$^1/_2$ tsp.**	**2 mL**
Garlic powder	**$^1/_8$ tsp.**	**0.5 mL**
Salt	**$^1/_4$ tsp.**	**1 mL**

Scramble-fry ground beef in non-stick skillet until no pink remains. Drain. Stir in taco seasoning and water. Simmer until all liquid is evaporated. Cool to room temperature. ■ Combine beans, lettuce, red pepper, onion and tomato in medium bowl. Toss together. Stir in beef mixture. ■ Fill tortilla bowls. ■ **Chili Dressing:** Combine all 6 ingredients in small bowl. Drizzle dressing over top.

Nutrition Information

1 cup (250 mL) salad only: 149 Calories; 12 g Protein; 3.7 g Total Fat (1.3 g Sat., 19.7 mg Cholesterol); 721 mg Sodium

Baste or brush foods with wine, oil-free marinade, low-fat dressing, broth or fruit juice instead of oil.

Tortilla Bowls

Make as many tortilla bowls as you need. The microwave method is better for corn tortillas—they tend to crack in the oven. Pictured on page 126.

Corn or flour tortilla, 6 or 7 inch (15 or 18 cm) size   1   1

Microwave Oven Method: Lightly grease bottom and outside of 2 cup (500 mL) microwave-safe liquid measure. 1. Turn measure upside down. Press tortilla over bottom and sides. Microwave on high (100%) power for 1 minute. 2. Using oven mitts, again press tortilla around measure. Microwave on high (100%) power for about 1 minute until brown spots begin to appear. Press tortilla against measure again, if necessary. 3. Turn out onto rack to cool.

Conventional Oven Method: Lightly grease bottom and outside of 2 cup (500 mL) oven-safe liquid measure. Turn measure upside down onto baking sheet. Press tortilla over bottom and sides. Bake in 325°F (160°C) oven for 7 to 10 minutes until brown spots appear, occasionally pressing tortilla against liquid measure.

Nutrition Information

1 tortilla bowl: 89 Calories; 3 g Protein; 1.5 g Total Fat (0 g Sat., 0 mg Cholesterol);
    71 mg Sodium

Note: For larger bowl, use 10 inch (25 cm) flour tortilla over 4 cup (1 L) liquid measure.

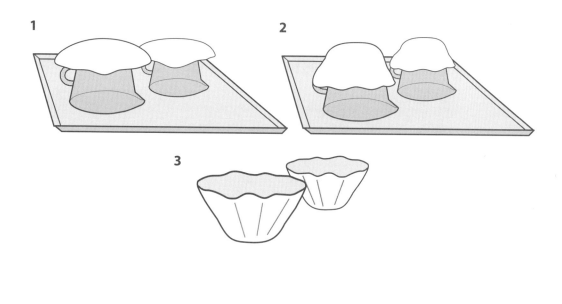

Mediterranean Salad

Preparation time is 40 minutes. This can be made the day before and refrigerated.
Makes 11 cups (2.75 L). Pictured on page 71.

Condensed chicken broth	**10 oz.**	**284 mL**
Water	**¹/₂ cup**	**125 mL**
Couscous	**1¹/₂ cups**	**375 mL**
Small red pepper, diced	**1**	**1**
Small yellow pepper, diced	**1**	**1**
Canned artichoke hearts, drained and quartered	**14 oz.**	**398 mL**
Canned chick peas (garbanzo beans), drained	**14 oz.**	**398 mL**
Green onions, sliced	**4**	**4**
Low-fat Cheddar cheese, cut into small cubes	**4 oz.**	**125 g**
Small celery stalks, thinly sliced	**2**	**2**
Chopped pitted ripe olives	**¹/₄ cup**	**60 mL**
Low-fat Italian dressing	**1 cup**	**250 mL**
Garlic clove, crushed	**1**	**1**
Grated lemon peel	**1 tsp.**	**5 mL**
Romaine lettuce leaves	**6-8**	**6-8**
Salt, to taste		
Pepper, to taste		

Combine chicken broth and water in saucepan. Bring to a boil. Remove from heat. Stir in couscous. Cover. Let stand for 15 to 20 minutes. ■ Toss next 8 ingredients together in large bowl. ■ Combine Italian dressing, garlic and lemon peel in small bowl. Pour over vegetable mixture. Add couscous. Toss lightly. Let stand for 2 hours. ■ Arrange lettuce leaves on bottom of platter or inside glass bowl. Spoon couscous mixture over lettuce.

Nutrition Information

1 cup (250 mL): 199 Calories; 10 g Protein; 4.1 g Total Fat (1.7 g Sat., 8.5 mg Cholesterol); 699 mg Sodium

Variation: Add 2 tbsp. (30 mL) chopped fresh sweet basil, mint or dill to dressing.

Tomato Pasta Salad

Preparation time is 30 minutes. Other pasta can be substituted. Makes 12 cups (3 L). Pictured on page 125.

Bow pasta, uncooked	**10 oz.**	**300 g**
Plum tomatoes, diced	**6**	**6**
Chopped fresh sweet basil, packed	**1/2 cup**	**125 mL**
Part-skim mozzarella cheese, cut into very small cubes	**4 oz.**	**125 g**
Sliced pitted ripe olives (optional)	**1/4 cup**	**60 mL**
TOMATO DRESSING		
Tomato juice	**1/2 cup**	**125 mL**
Red wine vinegar	**2 tbsp.**	**30 mL**
Olive oil	**1 tbsp.**	**15 mL**
Garlic cloves, minced	**2**	**2**
Worcestershire sauce	**1/2 tsp.**	**2 mL**
Salt	**1/2 tsp.**	**2 mL**
Freshly ground pepper	**1/8 tsp.**	**0.5 mL**

Cook pasta according to package directions. Drain. Rinse with cold water. ■ Combine tomato, basil, cheese and olives with pasta in large bowl. ■ **Tomato Dressing:** Combine all 7 ingredients in jar. Cover and shake. Pour over salad. Toss well. Let stand at room temperature for at least 30 minutes to allow flavors to blend.

Nutrition Information

1 cup (250 mL): 147 Calories; 7 g Protein; 3.5 g Total Fat (1.3 g Sat., 6.2 mg Cholesterol); 211 mg Sodium

. . . .

Serve salad dressing in a bowl with a small ladle or serving spoon; a smaller amount will likely be used than if pouring the dressing on.

Sauces

from pasta to dipping, these sauces offer a wide variety that can last the whole week through. Each one is under 3.5 grams of fat per serving, which means you can't go wrong in your selection! Go ahead and try a thick, creamy sauce—just when you thought you would never be able to splurge again!

Three Tomato Sauce

Uses three kinds of tomatoes-fresh, sun-dried and canned. Serve over pasta or Polenta Wedges, page 78. Makes 4 cups (1 L). Pictured on page 71.

Olive oil	1 tsp.	5 mL
Medium onion, chopped	1	1
Garlic clove, crushed	1	1
Sun-dried tomato halves, quartered	8	8
Canned roma tomatoes, put through food mill	2 × 14 oz.	2 × 398 mL
Finely chopped fresh sweet basil	$^1/_4$ cup	60 mL
Medium plum tomatoes, diced	3	3

Heat oil in large non-stick skillet. Sauté onion and garlic until onion is soft. ■ Add next 3 ingredients. Bring to a boil, stirring occasionally. ■ Add plum tomato. Stir. Simmer for 1 minute.

Nutrition Information

$^3/_4$ cup (175 mL): 82 Calories; 3 g Protein; 1.8 g Total Fat (0.3 g Sat., 0 mg Cholesterol); 264 mg Sodium

Roasted Pepper Sauce

As a variation, try this with yellow, orange or green peppers. Serve over whole wheat or flavored pasta. Makes 4$^1/_2$ cups (1.1 L) sauce, enough for 4 servings. Pictured on page 108.

Large red peppers	5	5
Chopped fresh sweet basil	$^2/_3$ **cup**	150 mL
Hard margarine	1 tsp.	5 mL
Garlic cloves, crushed	2	2
Green onions, sliced thinly	6	6
All-purpose flour	1$^1/_2$ **tbsp.**	25 mL
Skim evaporated milk	13$^1/_2$ **oz.**	385 mL
Dried oregano	$^1/_2$ **tsp.**	2 mL
Ground marjoram	$^1/_2$ **tsp.**	2 mL
Dried thyme	$^1/_2$ **tsp.**	2 mL
Salt	1$^1/_2$ **tsp.**	7 mL
Freshly ground pepper	$^1/_2$ **tsp.**	2 mL

Place peppers on baking sheet with sides. Broil 3 inches from heat for 30 minutes, turning several times until skin is blackened. Remove from oven. Cover with foil. Let stand until cool enough to handle. Peel off skin and discard seeds, reserving juice. ■ Put peeled pepper, reserved juice and basil into blender. Process until very finely chopped. ■ Melt margarine in non-stick skillet. Sauté garlic and green onion until onion is soft. ■ Combine flour and evaporated milk in small cup. Stir until smooth. Add oregano, marjoram, thyme, salt and pepper. Add to garlic mixture, along with pepper purée. Heat, stirring occasionally, until sauce is boiling and thickened. Serve immediately.

Nutrition Information

1 serving: 155 Calories; 11 g Protein; 1.6 g Total Fat (0.4 g Sat., 3.8 mg Cholesterol); 1162 mg Sodium

· ·

Use non-fat or low-fat salad dressing instead of sour cream, cheese, mayonnaise or other sauces over vegetables and in casseroles.

Black Bean Vegetable Sauce

Serve over pasta, rice or Polenta Wedges, page 78. Store in a covered container in the refrigerator for up to one week. Freezes well. Makes 5²/₃ cups (1.4 L). Pictured on page 108.

Olive oil	1 tsp.	5 mL
Garlic clove, minced	1	1
Medium carrots, thinly sliced	2	2
Medium yellow pepper, diced	1	1
Medium onion, coarsely chopped	1	1
Medium tomatoes, diced	2	2
Canned crushed tomatoes	14 oz.	398 mL
Dried oregano	1 tsp.	5 mL
Granulated sugar	2 tsp.	10 mL
Hot pepper sauce	¹/₄ tsp.	1 mL
Canned black beans, well-drained	19 oz.	540 mL

Heat oil in large non-stick wok or skillet. Sauté garlic. Add carrot, pepper and onion. Stir-fry for 4 minutes. ■ Add tomato. Stir-fry for 2 minutes. Add remaining 5 ingredients. Stir. Simmer for 10 minutes.

Nutrition Information

³/₄ cup (175 mL): 93 Calories; 4 g Protein; 1.1 g Total Fat (0.2 g Sat., 0 mg Cholesterol); 183 mg Sodium

Creamy Dijon Spinach Sauce

Serve over pasta or Polenta Wedges, page 78. Garnish with freshly ground pepper and pimiento. Makes 4 cups (1 L) sauce. Pictured on page 108 and on the front cover.

Olive oil	2 tsp.	10 mL
Small onion, coarsely chopped	1	1
Garlic cloves, minced	2	2
Coarsely chopped spinach	4 cups	1 L
Water	1 cup	250 mL
Chicken bouillon powder	1¹/₂ tsp.	7 mL
Dried rosemary, crushed	¹/₄ tsp.	1 mL
Dried thyme	¹/₄ tsp.	1 mL
Dried sweet basil	¹/₄ tsp.	1 mL
Dijon mustard	1 tbsp.	15 mL
All-purpose flour	1 tbsp.	15 mL
Cornstarch	1 tbsp.	15 mL
Skim evaporated milk	1 cup	250 mL

(continued on next page)

Heat oil in non-stick skillet. Sauté onion and garlic until onion is soft. Add spinach. Sauté for 1 minute. ■ Add next 6 ingredients. Bring to a boil. Reduce heat. Simmer, uncovered, for 5 minutes. ■ Combine flour and cornstarch in small bowl. Gradually whisk in evaporated milk. Add spinach mixture. Mix well. Bring to a boil. Reduce heat. Simmer for 1 minute until slightly thickened.

Nutrition Information

1 cup (250 mL): 117 Calories; 8 g Protein; 3.1 g Total Fat (0.5 g Sat., 2.6 mg Cholesterol); 422 mg Sodium

Shiitake Wine Sauce

To keep mushrooms fresh, store in a paper bag in the refrigerator. Do not rinse mushrooms until ready to use. Serve sauce over chicken, fish or pasta. Makes 2 cups (500 mL). Pictured on page 108.

Hard margarine	1 tbsp.	15 mL
Garlic cloves, minced	2	2
Finely chopped shallots	$^1/_3$ cup	75 mL
Thinly sliced shiitake mushrooms, stems removed	3 cups	750 mL
Water	1 cup	250 mL
Chicken bouillon powder	$1^1/_2$ tsp.	7 mL
Dry white wine	$^1/_2$ cup	125 mL
Finely chopped fresh dill	1 tbsp.	15 mL
Freshly ground pepper	$^1/_4$ tsp.	1 mL
All-purpose flour	2 tbsp.	30 mL
Skim evaporated milk	1 cup	250 mL

Melt margarine in medium saucepan until bubbling. Sauté garlic and shallots for 1 to 2 minutes until shallots are soft. Add mushrooms. Sauté for 5 minutes until soft. ■ Stir in water, bouillon powder and wine. Bring to a boil. Reduce heat. Simmer, uncovered, for 10 minutes until slightly reduced. Remove from heat. Stir in dill and ground pepper. ■ Combine flour and evaporated milk. Whisk until smooth. Stir into mushroom mixture. Return to heat. Bring to a boil. Boil until slightly thickened. Serve immediately.

Nutrition Information

$^1/_2$ cup (125 mL): 193 Calories; 8 g Protein; 3.5 g Total Fat (0.8 g Sat., 2.6 mg Cholesterol); 363 mg Sodium

Plum Sauce

Stir this sauce constantly to prevent it from burning. Serve with Baked Spring Rolls, page 11, or Chicken Fingers, page 19. Makes 1 1/3 cups (325 mL). Pictured on page 17.

Strained plums or prunes (baby food)	**2 × 4 1/2 oz.**	**2 × 128 mL**
White vinegar	**2 tbsp.**	**30 mL**
Brown sugar, packed	**1/4 cup**	**60 mL**
Freshly squeezed orange juice	**2 tbsp.**	**30 mL**
Grated orange peel	**1/4 tsp.**	**1 mL**
Dry mustard powder	**1/2 tsp.**	**2 mL**
Ground ginger	**1/4 tsp.**	**1 mL**
Ground allspice	**1/8 tsp.**	**0.5 mL**

Combine all 8 ingredients in small saucepan. Bring mixture to a boil, stirring constantly. Boil until sugar is dissolved. Cool before serving to allow flavors to blend.

Nutrition Information

1 tbsp. (15 mL): 20 Calories; trace Protein; trace Total Fat (0 g Sat., 0 mg Cholesterol);
2 mg Sodium

Fresh Mango Chutney

Cover and store in the refrigerator for up to five days. Makes 2 cups (500 mL).

Fresh ripe mangos, peeled and finely chopped	**2**	**2**
Juice of 1 medium lime		
Juice and grated peel of 1 large orange		
Cider vinegar	**1/4 cup**	**60 mL**
Freshly grated gingerroot	**2 tsp.**	**10 mL**
Brown sugar, packed	**2 tsp.**	**10 mL**
Dried crushed chilies	**1/4 tsp.**	**1 mL**
Curry powder	**1/4 tsp.**	**1 mL**
Salt	**1/4 tsp.**	**1 mL**

Combine all 9 ingredients in medium bowl. Let stand for 30 minutes at room temperature.

Nutrition Information

1 tbsp. (15 mL): 12 Calories; trace Protein; trace Total Fat (trace g Sat., 0 mg Cholesterol);
21 mg Sodium

Soups

very recipe here has less than 2.5 grams of fat per serving—perfect for lunch or dinner! Skim evaporated milk works well as a delicious substitution for heavy cream when preparing a creamed soup. Share these mouthwatering recipes with your family and friends.

Garlic And Onion Soup

This soup is best served the same day. Preparation time is only 20 minutes. Makes 7 cups (1.75 L). Pictured on page 71.

Olive oil	1 tbsp.	15 mL
Large onion, very thinly sliced and slivered	1	1
Garlic cloves, minced	8	8
Apple juice	3 tbsp.	50 mL
All-purpose flour	1 tbsp.	15 mL
White wine	¹/₂ cup	125 mL
Water	7 cups	1.75 L
Beef bouillon powder	2 tsp.	10 mL
Bay leaves	2	2
Hot pepper sauce, dash		
Chopped fresh parsley	2 tbsp.	30 mL
Salt	2 tsp.	10 mL
Pepper	¹/₈ tsp.	0.5 mL
Tri-colored fusilli or other spiral pasta	1¹/₂ cups	375 mL
Liquid gravy browner (such as Kitchen Bouquet)	1¹/₂ tsp.	7 mL

Heat oil in non-stick skillet. Sauté onion and garlic for 5 minutes. Add apple juice. Reduce heat to low. Cover. Cook, stirring occasionally, until onion is very soft and golden. ■ Sprinkle with flour. Mix well. Transfer to large Dutch oven. Stir in wine. Add next 7 ingredients. Bring to a boil. ■ Add pasta. Simmer until pasta is tender. Stir in gravy browner.

Nutrition Information

1 cup (250 mL): 123 Calories; 3 g Protein; 2.4 g Total Fat (0.4 g Sat., 0.1 mg Cholesterol); 1046 mg Sodium

Orzo Mushroom Soup

Orzo (OHR-zoh) in Italian means "barley." It is actually a tiny, rice-shaped pasta. Use a variety of mushrooms for more flavor. Makes 9 cups (2.25 L). Pictured on page 72.

Fresh mushrooms, finely chopped	1¹/₂ **lbs.**	**680 g**
All-purpose flour	**3 tbsp.**	**50 mL**
Garlic cloves, minced	**3**	**3**
Water	**6 cups**	**1.5 L**
Beef bouillon powder	**3 tbsp.**	**50 mL**
Green onions, thinly sliced	**3**	**3**
Salt	**1 tsp.**	**5 mL**
Freshly ground pepper	¹/₂**-1 tsp.**	**2-5 mL**
Orzo pasta, uncooked	¹/₂ **cup**	**125 mL**
Non-fat sour cream	**1 cup**	**250 mL**

Heat lightly greased large Dutch oven until hot. Sauté mushrooms, flour and garlic for 5 minutes. ■ Add water, bouillon powder, green onion, salt and pepper. Simmer for 15 minutes. ■ Add orzo. Simmer for 10 minutes. Remove from heat. Stir in sour cream.

N u t r i t i o n   I n f o r m a t i o n

1 cup (250 mL): 67 Calories; 4 g Protein; 0.8 g Total Fat (0.2 g Sat., 0.4 mg Cholesterol); 911 mg Sodium

Bean And Vegetable Soup

Use any type of canned beans. Preparation time is 20 minutes. Makes 11 cups (2.75 L). Pictured on page 72.

Diet tub margarine	**1 tbsp.**	**15 mL**
Medium onion, diced	**1**	**1**
Celery stalk, chopped	**1**	**1**
Water	**6 cups**	**1.5 L**
Vegetable bouillon powder	**2 tbsp.**	**30 mL**
Coarsely chopped cabbage	**2 cups**	**500 mL**
Diced carrot	**1 cup**	**250 mL**
Canned diced tomatoes, with juice	**14 oz.**	**398 mL**
Canned navy beans, with liquid	**14 oz.**	**398 mL**
Medium potato, diced	**1**	**1**
Dried crushed chilies	¹/₄ **tsp.**	**1 mL**
Chopped fresh parsley	**1 tbsp.**	**15 mL**
Freshly ground pepper	¹/₈ **tsp.**	**0.5 mL**

(continued on next page)

Melt margarine in large Dutch oven. Sauté onion and celery until soft. ■ Add remaining 10 ingredients. Cover. Simmer for 40 minutes until vegetables are tender.

1 cup (250 mL): 81 Calories; 4 g Protein; 1.3 g Total Fat (0.3 g Sat., trace Cholesterol); 239 mg Sodium

Comfort Corn Chowder

Chowders are thick, rich soups containing chunks of vegetables. Makes 10 cups (2.5 L). Pictured on page 72.

Diet tub margarine	1 tbsp.	15 mL
Medium onion, chopped	1	1
Celery stalk, chopped	1	1
Chopped green pepper	$^1/_2$ cup	125 mL
Canned kernel corn, with liquid, slightly mashed	2 × 12 oz.	2 × 341 mL
Medium potatoes, peeled and diced	3	3
Water	3 cups	750 mL
Hot pepper sauce	$^1/_8$ tsp.	0.5 mL
Chili powder	$^1/_2$ tsp.	2 mL
Salt	$1^1/_2$ tsp.	7 mL
Pepper	$^1/_4$ tsp.	1 mL
All-purpose flour	$^1/_4$ cup	60 mL
Skim evaporated milk	$13^1/_2$ oz.	385 mL
Chopped fresh parsley	$1^1/_2$ tsp.	7 mL
Bacon slice, cooked crisp and crumbled (optional)	1	1

Melt margarine in large Dutch oven. Sauté onion, celery and green pepper. ■ Add next 7 ingredients. Bring to a boil. Reduce heat. Simmer for 15 minutes until potatoes are tender. ■ Combine flour and evaporated milk in small bowl. Stir until smooth. Add to corn mixture. Add parsley and bacon. Bring to a boil, stirring until thickened.

1 cup (250 mL): 133 Calories; 6 g Protein; 1.1 g Total Fat (0.2 g Sat., 1.5 mg Cholesterol); 634 mg Sodium

Roasted Onion And Garlic Bisque

Use Vidalia or Walla Walla sweet onions. To freeze this soup, make without the evaporated milk.
Add the milk once the soup is thawed. Heat and serve. Makes 8 cups (2 L). Pictured on page 72.

Large head of garlic	1	1
Large white onions, cut into wedges	4-5	4-5
Olive oil (or use cooking spray)	2 tsp.	10 mL
Olive oil	1 tsp.	5 mL
Medium leeks, thinly sliced	2	2
All-purpose flour	2 tbsp.	30 mL
Dried thyme	1 tsp.	5 mL
Salt	1 tsp.	5 mL
Condensed chicken broth	2 × 10 oz.	2 × 284 mL
Dry white wine	¹/₃ **cup**	75 mL
Skim evaporated milk	2 × 13¹/₂ oz.	2 × 385 mL
Non-fat sour cream, for garnish		

Remove loose outer covering on garlic without separating cloves. Place garlic and onion on lightly greased baking sheet. Lightly brush surface of garlic and onion with first amount of oil. Bake in 350°F (175°C) oven for 1 hour. Cool. ■ Heat second amount of oil in large Dutch oven. Sauté leeks for 20 minutes until soft and golden. Sprinkle with flour, thyme and salt. Stir well. Stir in chicken broth. ■ Squeeze garlic pulp into blender. Add onion. Process. Gradually add white wine, processing until smooth. Pour into leek mixture. Simmer for 30 minutes. Remove from heat. ■ Stir in evaporated milk. Heat gently until hot. Do not boil. ■ Garnish with dollop of sour cream.

N u t r i t i o n I n f o r m a t i o n

1 cup (250 mL): 190 Calories; 13 g Protein; 3 g Total Fat (0.6 g Sat., 4.5 mg Cholesterol); 941 mg Sodium

To make creamy soup without using cream, purée the vegetable mixture in a blender or food processor or use skim evaporated milk.

Stir-Fries

ast, fresh and healthy—stir-frying is great for today's lifestyle. If you heat your skillet or wok until hot and then add your oil, you will be able to use less oil while cooking. Enjoy the fresh, new taste of these stir-fries.

Spicy Beef And Bean Sprouts

It is easier to slice the beef when it is slightly frozen. Serve over hot rice. Makes 6 cups (1.5 L). Pictured on page 143.

Eye of round steak	$^3/_4$ **lb.**	**340 g**
Low-fat vegetable or chicken bouillon cube	$^1/_4 \times ^1/_3$ **oz.**	$^1/_4 \times$ **10.5 g**
Warm water	$^1/_2$ **cup**	**125 mL**
Chili sauce	**1 tbsp.**	**15 mL**
Garlic clove, minced	**1**	**1**
Low-sodium soy sauce	**2 tbsp.**	**30 mL**
Freshly grated gingerroot	**1 tsp.**	**5 mL**
Dried crushed chilies	$^1/_4$ **tsp.**	**1 mL**
Granulated sugar	$^1/_4$ **tsp.**	**1 mL**
Medium carrots, cut julienne	**2**	**2**
Medium onion, cut lengthwise into slivers	**1**	**1**
Fresh bean sprouts	**3 cups**	**750 mL**
Cornstarch	**2 tsp.**	**10 mL**
Reserved marinade, plus water to make	$^2/_3$ **cup**	**150 mL**

Cut steak along grain into thin 2 inch (5 cm) strips. Cut strips across grain into $^1/_8$ inch (3 mm) julienne strips. Combine next 8 ingredients in medium bowl. Stir well. Pour over steak in deep bowl. Marinate for 15 minutes. ■ Lightly grease non-stick wok or skillet and heat until hot. Remove steak from marinade to wok with slotted spoon, reserving marinade. Stir-fry for 2 minutes until beef is no longer pink. Remove to bowl. This may need to be done in 2 batches. Add carrot and onion to wok. Stir-fry for 3 minutes. Add bean sprouts. Stir-fry for 2 minutes. Return beef to wok. ■ Stir cornstarch into reserved marinade. Add reserved marinade and water to steak mixture. Stir until hot and **thickened.**

Nutrition Information

1 cup (250 mL): 103 Calories; 14 g Protein; 1.6 g Total Fat (0.5 g Sat., 20.8 mg Cholesterol); 328 mg Sodium

Ginger Orange Pork

Rice wine is a sweet, golden wine made from fermenting rice. Most are low in alcohol. Serves 6.

Pork loin, trimmed of fat	$^3/_4$ **lb.**	**340 g**
Juice and grated peel of 1 orange		
Freshly minced gingerroot	1 tbsp.	15 mL
Garlic clove, finely minced	1	1
Liquid honey	2 tsp.	10 mL
Low-sodium soy sauce	1 tbsp.	15 mL
Rice wine (such as sake)	3 tbsp.	50 mL
Julienned carrot	2 cups	500 mL
Fresh pea pods (or frozen, thawed)	2 cups	500 mL
Green onions, quartered lengthwise and cut into 2 inch (5 cm) slices	4	4
Canned sliced water chestnuts, drained	8 oz.	227 mL

Cut pork into ¹/₄ inch (6 mm) strips. Cut strips crosswise into 3 inch (7.5 cm) slices. Combine pork with orange juice, orange peel, ginger, garlic, honey, soy sauce and rice wine. Marinate for 30 minutes, stirring occasionally. ■ Heat non-stick wok or skillet until hot. Add pork with marinade. Stir-fry for 5 minutes until pork is no longer pink. Remove to bowl with slotted spoon. Add carrot and pea pods to wok. Stir-fry for 3 minutes. Add green onion and water chestnuts. Stir-fry for 2 minutes. Add pork. Stir until hot. Serve over rice.

Nutrition Information

1 serving: 149 Calories; 15 g Protein; 1.7 g Total Fat (0.5 g Sat., 32 mg Cholesterol); 152 mg Sodium

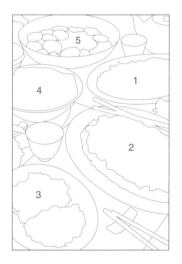

Italian Squash Stir-Fry

Spoon over rice or pasta or use as a vegetable accompaniment with any meat dish. Serves 6. Pictured on page 143.

Olive oil	**1 tbsp.**	**15 mL**

Small green or yellow zucchini,
    cut in half lengthwise and cut
    crosswise into $^1/_2$ **inch (12 mm) slices**
	4	**4**

Large red onion, slivered lengthwise	**1**	**1**
Thinly sliced fresh sweet basil	$^1/_4$ **cup**	**60 mL**
Garlic clove, minced	**1**	**1**
Salt	**1 tsp.**	**5 mL**
Freshly ground pepper	$^1/_8$ **tsp.**	**0.5 mL**
Large plum tomatoes, sliced	**6**	**6**
Grated part-skim mozzarella cheese	**1 cup**	**250 mL**
Grated fresh Parmesan cheese (optional)		

Heat oil in large non-stick wok or skillet until hot. Stir-fry zucchini with onion for 3 to 5 minutes until tender-crisp. Stir in basil, garlic, salt and pepper. ■ Spread zucchini mixture evenly in bottom of wok. Lay tomato over zucchini. Sprinkle with mozzarella cheese. Cook for 2 minutes until cheese is melted. Do not stir. Garnish with Parmesan cheese.

N u t r i t i o n   I n f o r m a t i o n

1 serving: 123 Calories; 7 g Protein; 6.1 g Total Fat (2.5 g Sat., 11.8 mg Cholesterol); 562 mg Sodium

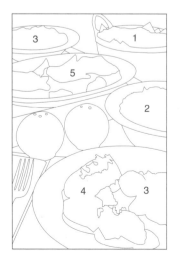

1. Crispy Sweet Potato, page 153
2. Tabbouleh, page 118
3. Tangy Roasted Veggies, page 154
4. Crab-Stuffed Chicken With Parsley Sauce, page 97
5. Gourmet Fish Steaks, page 99

Fish In Black Bean Sauce

Serve over a bed of rice. Makes 6 cups (1.5 L). Pictured on page 143.

Sesame oil	1 tsp.	5 mL
Firm white flesh fish (such as cod or halibut), cut bite size	1 lb.	454 g
Medium onion, slivered lengthwise	1	1
Garlic clove, minced	1	1
Freshly minced gingerroot	2 tsp.	10 mL
Large green, red, yellow or orange peppers, cut into chunks	2	2
Sliced fresh mushrooms	2 cups	500 mL
Fresh pea pods (or frozen, thawed)	2 cups	500 mL
Black bean sauce	¹/₄ cup	60 mL
Cold water	1 tbsp.	15 mL
Low-sodium soy sauce	1 tbsp.	15 mL
Granulated sugar	2 tsp.	10 mL
Cornstarch	2 tsp.	10 mL

Heat oil in large non-stick wok or skillet until hot. Add fish. Stir-fry for 2 minutes. Add onion, garlic and ginger. Stir-fry for 2 to 3 minutes until onion is soft. Remove to bowl with slotted spoon. Boil remaining liquid until reduced to ¹/₄ cup (60 mL). ■ Add peppers, mushrooms and pea pods. Stir-fry for 1 minute. ■ Combine black bean sauce, water, soy sauce, sugar and cornstarch in small cup. Pour over vegetables. Stir-fry for 3 to 4 minutes until vegetables are tender-crisp and sauce is thickened. Add fish and onion. Stir gently.

Nutrition Information

1 cup (250 mL): 138 Calories; 17 g Protein; 2.4 g Total Fat (0.3 g Sat., 32.5 mg Cholesterol); 616 mg Sodium

To enhance flavor and tenderize lean meat, marinate in savory mixtures for a few hours before cooking. You don't have to add oil to the mixture.

Vegetable Stir-Fry

Ask family members to join in to help speed up the process. Cooking time is less than 10 minutes! Serves 4. Pictured on page 143.

Low-fat vegetable or chicken bouillon cube	1 x $^1/_3$ oz.	1 x 10.5 g
Boiling water	1 cup	250 mL
Garlic cloves, minced	2	2
Thinly sliced carrot	$^1/_2$ cup	125 mL
Thinly sliced broccoli stem	1 cup	250 mL
Broccoli florets	2 cups	500 mL
Fresh pea pods, trimmed	4 oz.	125 g
Large red onion, sliced lengthwise into wedges	1	1
Cornstarch	2 tbsp.	30 mL
Low-sodium soy sauce	2 tbsp.	30 mL

Dissolve bouillon cube in boiling water in small cup. Heat $^1/_2$ cup (125 mL) broth in large non-stick wok or skillet until boiling. Add garlic, carrot and broccoli stems. Stir-fry for 3 minutes until vegetables are tender-crisp. ■ Add broccoli florets and pea pods. Stir-fry for 2 minutes. Add onion. Stir-fry for 1 minute. ■ Combine remaining $^1/_2$ cup (125 mL) broth, cornstarch and soy sauce in small bowl. Mix until smooth. Add to vegetable mixture. Stir-fry for 1 minute until thickened.

Nutrition Information

1 serving: 81 Calories; 5 g Protein; 0.7 g Total Fat (0.2 g Sat., 0 mg Cholesterol); 828 mg Sodium

Use wine, lemon juice or broth instead of butter or margarine when sautéing or stir-frying. If using oil, cut down on the fat needed to stir-fry by putting oil in an already heated skillet. A little will go further and the food will absorb less.

Pineapple Pork

Rice flour is used in this recipe to make the pork chops crisp. All-purpose flour can be substituted, although a less crispy product will result. Makes 5 cups (1.2 L). Pictured on page 143.

Boneless pork loin chops, fat removed	12 oz.	340 g
Egg white (large), fork-beaten	1	1
Lemon juice, fresh or bottled	1 tsp.	5 mL
Rice flour	$^1/_3$ cup	75 mL
Cornstarch	2 tsp.	10 mL
Thinly sliced baby carrots	1 cup	250 mL
Canned pineapple tidbits, with juice	19 oz.	540 mL
Prepared pineapple or orange juice	1 cup	250 mL
White vinegar	1 tbsp.	15 mL
Brown sugar, packed	2 tbsp.	30 mL
Ketchup	2 tbsp.	30 mL
Ground ginger	1 tsp.	5 mL
Salt	$^1/_4$ tsp.	1 mL
Medium green pepper, cut in slivers	1	1
Cornstarch	2 tsp.	10 mL
Water	2 tsp.	10 mL

Slice pork chops crosswise into $^1/_2$ inch (12 mm) strips. Combine egg white and lemon juice in medium bowl. Add pork strips and coat well. Stir rice flour and first amount of cornstarch together. Sift over pork, tossing with fork until pork is well coated. Lightly grease non-stick wok or skillet. Sauté pork, in 2 batches, until lightly browned. ■ Add next 8 ingredients. Cover. Simmer for 30 to 40 minutes. Add green pepper. Cover. Simmer for 5 minutes until green pepper is tender-crisp. ■ Stir second amount of cornstarch and water together in small cup. Slowly stir into vegetable mixture until thickened.

Nutrition Information

1 cup (250 mL): 288 Calories; 17 g Protein; 4.2 g Total Fat (1.4 g Sat., 38.6 mg Cholesterol); 282 mg Sodium

Use a non-stick skillet or wok, or use no-stick cooking spray, in place of butter, margarine or oil when frying meat or vegetables.

Vegetables

e always tend to think of vegetables as low-fat, so why include them in *Low-Fat Cooking*? Because there are some wonderful and different ways of preparing vegetables, such as roasting and frying, that can complement any main course or luncheon fare.

Confetti Cauliflower Casserole

This is great reheated the next day. Serves 6. Pictured on page 89.

Evaporated skim milk	13¹/₂ oz.	385 mL
All-purpose flour	¹/₄ cup	60 mL
Cornstarch	1 tbsp.	15 mL
Garlic powder	¹/₄ tsp.	1 mL
Low-fat chicken-flavored bouillon cube	1 × ¹/₃ oz.	1 × 10.5 g
Finely diced red pepper	¹/₂ cup	125 mL
Salt	1 tsp.	5 mL
White pepper	¹/₈ tsp.	0.5 mL
Sliced green onion	¹/₂ cup	125 mL
Cauliflower florets, cooked and drained well	5 cups	1.25 L
Crisp rice cereal (such as Special K)	1 cup	250 mL
Grated low-fat Cheddar cheese	¹/₂ cup	125 mL

Combine evaporated milk, flour and cornstarch in jar. Cover and shake. Pour into saucepan. Add next 5 ingredients and stir until thickened. Stir in green onion.
■ Place cauliflower in lightly greased 2 quart (2 L) casserole dish. Pour sauce over cauliflower and lightly fold until well combined. ■ Sprinkle top with cereal and cheese. Bake, uncovered, in 350°F (175°C) oven for about 20 minutes until heated through and cheese is melted.

Nutrition Information

1 serving: 164 Calories; 12 g Protein; 2.8 g Total Fat (1.5 g Sat., 8.5 mg Cholesterol); 985 mg Sodium

Potato And Roasted Garlic Casserole

To save energy, roast the garlic in the oven while you are baking another dish. Makes 5 cups (1.25 L).

Head of garlic	1	1
Peeled and cooked medium potatoes	6	6
Diet tub margarine	2 tbsp.	30 mL
Skim evaporated milk	1/4 cup	60 mL
Salt	1/2 tsp.	2 mL
Pepper	1/4 tsp.	1 mL
Canola oil (or use cooking spray)	1/2 tsp.	2 mL
Paprika, sprinkle		

Cut thin slice off root end of whole garlic, exposing all cloves. Wrap garlic in foil. Bake in 400°F (205°C) oven for 1 hour. Let cool enough to handle. Squeeze pulp out of garlic from cut end. ■ Combine warm potatoes, margarine, milk and roasted garlic pulp in large bowl. Beat on low until smooth. Sprinkle with salt and pepper. Spread into lightly greased 2 quart (2 L) casserole dish. Lightly oil surface of potato. ■ Sprinkle with paprika. Bake in 350°F (175°C) oven for 30 minutes until heated through.

Nutrition Information

1 cup (250 mL): 188 Calories; 4 g Protein; 3 g Total Fat (0.5 g Sat., 0.5 mg Cholesterol); 326 mg Sodium

Mixed Vegetable Wok

No sauce is needed. Simply fresh crisp vegetables. Makes 4 cups (1 L). Pictured on page 90.

Condensed chicken broth (10 oz., 284 mL)	1/2 cup	125 mL
Garlic clove, crushed	1	1
Carrots, thinly sliced on the diagonal	2	2
Sliced fresh green beans, 1 inch (2.5 cm) pieces	1 1/2 cups	375 mL
Medium onion, cut lengthwise into slivers	1	1
Fresh pea pods, trimmed	1 cup	250 mL
Whole or sliced small fresh mushrooms	2 cups	500 mL
Cornstarch	2 tsp.	10 mL
Water	2 tbsp.	30 mL

(continued on next page)

Heat chicken broth in large non-stick wok until bubbling. Add garlic, carrot and green beans. Stir-fry for 7 minutes. ■ Add onion, pea pods and mushrooms. Stir-fry for 3 to 4 minutes until vegetables are tender-crisp. ■ Combine cornstarch and water in small cup. Add to vegetables. Stir-fry for 2 minutes until thickened.

Nutrition Information

1 cup (250 mL): 84 Calories; 5 g Protein; 0.8 g Total Fat (0.2 g Sat., 0.3 mg Cholesterol); 228 mg Sodium

Baked Potato Pancakes

Use a tea towel to squeeze all the liquid out of the grated raw potato. Bake the potato pancakes as soon as the mixture is combined. The raw potato will turn brown quickly if left sitting. Makes 14 potato pancakes.

Small onion, diced	1	1
Garlic clove, minced	1	1
Large eggs, fork-beaten	2	2
Salt	1$^1/_2$ tsp.	7 mL
Freshly ground pepper	$^1/_8$-$^1/_4$ tsp.	0.5-1 mL
Medium potatoes, peeled and grated	4	4
Corn flake crumbs	$^1/_4$ cup	60 mL
All-purpose flour	2 tbsp.	30 mL
Baking powder	$^1/_2$ tsp.	2 mL

Combine onion and garlic in blender or food processor. Pulse until very finely chopped. Pour into large bowl. Combine eggs, salt and pepper. Add to onion mixture. ■ Squeeze any liquid out of potato. Add potato to onion mixture. ■ Combine corn flake crumbs, flour and baking powder. Mix into potato mixture. For each pancake, spoon $^1/_4$ cup (60 mL) potato mixture onto lightly greased baking sheets. Flatten with spatula. Bake in 450°F (230°C) oven for 12 minutes. Flip potato pancakes over. Bake for 7 minutes until browned and crispy.

Nutrition Information

1 potato pancake: 49 Calories; 2 g Protein; 0.8 g Total Fat (0.2 g Sat., 30.8 mg Cholesterol); 320 mg Sodium

Zucchini Patties

Use up all the zucchini in your garden making these. Makes 12 patties. Pictured on page 89.

Grated zucchini, with peel	**3 cups**	**750 mL**
Finely chopped onion	**$^1/_4$ cup**	**60 mL**
Sun-dried tomato halves, softened in boiling water for 10 minutes, chopped	**5**	**5**
Egg whites (large), fork-beaten	**2**	**2**
Dry fine bread crumbs	**$^2/_3$ cup**	**150 mL**
Low-fat salad dressing (or mayonnaise)	**1 tbsp.**	**15 mL**
Whole wheat flour	**2 tbsp.**	**30 mL**
Garlic clove, minced	**1**	**1**
Dried oregano	**$^1/_8$ tsp.**	**0.5 mL**
Dried sweet basil	**$^1/_8$ tsp.**	**0.5 mL**
Salt	**$^1/_2$ tsp.**	**2 mL**
Pepper	**$^1/_8$ tsp.**	**0.5 mL**

Combine all 12 ingredients in large bowl. Mix well to moisten bread crumbs. Form into patties, using $^1/_4$ cup (60 mL) for each. Heat lightly greased non-stick skillet until hot. Cook patties for 3 to 4 minutes per side until crisp and golden.

N u t r i t i o n   I n f o r m a t i o n

1 patty: 51 Calories; 3 g Protein; 0.8 g Total Fat (0.1 g Sat., 0.1 mg Cholesterol); 183 mg Sodium

Sauerkraut And Potato Casserole

Sauerkraut is German for "sour cabbage." It is actually a Chinese creation from over 2,000 years ago. It was fermented with rice wine, and now is fermented with salt and spices. Makes 6 cups (1.5 L).

Chicken bouillon powder	**$^3/_4$ tsp.**	**4 mL**
Water	**$^1/_2$ cup**	**125 mL**
Chopped onion	**1 cup**	**250 mL**
Canned sauerkraut, drained	**16 oz.**	**500 mL**
Caraway seed (optional)	**1 tsp.**	**5 mL**
Mashed or riced potato	**4 cups**	**1 L**
Skim milk	**$^1/_2$ cup**	**125 mL**
Salt	**$^1/_2$ tsp.**	**2 mL**
Pepper	**$^1/_4$ tsp.**	**1 mL**
Dry bread crumbs	**$^1/_4$ cup**	**60 mL**
Grated low-fat Cheddar cheese	**$^1/_2$ cup**	**125 mL**
Paprika, sprinkle		

(continued on next page)

Heat bouillon powder and water in large non-stick skillet. Sauté onion in broth until soft and most of liquid is evaporated. ■ Add sauerkraut. Stir-fry for 5 minutes. Add caraway seed. ■ Mix potato, milk, salt and pepper in bowl. Stir in sauerkraut and onion. Place in lightly greased 2 quart (2 L) casserole dish. Smooth top. ■ Combine bread crumbs and cheese. Sprinkle over casserole. Sprinkle with paprika. Bake in 350°F (175°C) oven for 30 minutes until hot.

Nutrition Information

1 cup (250 mL): 226 Calories; 8 g Protein; 2.6 g Total Fat (1.4 g Sat., 6.5 mg Cholesterol); 811 mg Sodium

Crispy Sweet Potato

The pale sweet potato has thin light yellow skin and pale yellow flesh. It is not sweet after it is baked. The darker sweet potato has thicker, dark orange skin and sweet orange flesh that cooks to a moist texture. Serves 4. Pictured on page 144.

Egg whites, large (or ¹/₄ cup, 60 mL, egg white substitute such as Simply Egg Whites)	**3**	**3**
Garlic powder	**¹/₂ tsp.**	**2 mL**
Crushed corn flakes cereal	**¹/₂ cup**	**125 mL**
Grated light Parmesan cheese product	**¹/₄ cup**	**60 mL**
Dried parsley flakes	**1 tsp.**	**5 mL**
Dried sweet basil	**1 tsp.**	**5 mL**
Sweet potatoes (white or orange), with peel, cut into ¹/₂ inch (12 mm) slices	**1¹/₂ lbs.**	**680 g**

Beat egg whites and garlic powder together in small bowl. ■ Combine cereal, Parmesan cheese, parsley and basil in pie plate. ■ Dip each potato slice into egg mixture and then into cereal mixture. Coat well. Place slices on lightly greased 11 x 17 inch (28 x 43 cm) baking sheet. Bake in 425°F (220°C) oven for 20 minutes. Turn slices over. Bake for 10 minutes until tender.

Nutrition Information

1 serving: 259 Calories; 12 g Protein; 1.5 g Total Fat (0.7 g Sat., 2.6 mg Cholesterol); 302 mg Sodium

Variation: Substitute baking potatoes for sweet potatoes.

Tangy Roasted Veggies

Serve warm, or as a cold vegetable salad. Makes 8 cups (2 L). Pictured on page 144 and on the front cover.

Cut fresh green beans, 1 inch (2.5 cm) pieces	2 cups	500 mL
Sliced baby carrots, cut on the diagonal into $^1/_2$ inch (12 mm) slices	1 cup	250 mL
Red pepper, cut into $1^1/_2$ inch (3.8 cm) pieces	1	1
Yellow pepper, cut into $1^1/_2$ inch (3.8 cm) pieces	1	1
Small new potatoes, quartered	2 lbs.	900 g
Low-fat Italian dressing	$^1/_2$ cup	125 mL
Salt	$^1/_2$ tsp.	2 mL
Pepper	$^1/_4$ tsp.	1 mL
Head of garlic	1	1
Balsamic vinegar	$^1/_3$ cup	75 mL
Olive oil	1 tbsp.	15 mL
Dried rosemary, crushed	$^1/_2$ tsp.	2 mL
Sliced green onion	$^1/_2$ cup	125 mL
Chopped fresh parsley, for garnish	2 tbsp.	30 mL

Blanch green beans in boiling water for 1 minute. Rinse under cold water. Drain. Place in small bowl. ■ Combine next 4 ingredients in large bowl. Stir in Italian dressing, salt and pepper. Put vegetables onto lightly greased large baking sheet. ■ Cut thin slice off root end of whole garlic, exposing all cloves. Place cut side up in center of vegetables. Bake in 400°F (205°C) oven for 45 minutes. Add green beans. Bake for 15 minutes until potatoes are tender. Remove vegetables to large bowl. ■ Squeeze pulp of roasted garlic into small bowl. Stir in vinegar, oil, rosemary and green onion. Mix well. Pour over vegetables. ■ Garnish with parsley.

Nutrition Information

1 cup (250 mL): 179 Calories; 4 g Protein; 2.5 g Total Fat (0.3 g Sat., 1 mg Cholesterol); 414 mg Sodium

Make steamed vegetables as tasty as they are nutritious by choosing the freshest possible.

Measurement Tables

Throughout this book measurements are given in Conventional and Metric measure. To compensate for differences between the two measurements due to rounding, a full metric measure is not always used. The cup used is the standard 8 fluid ounce. Temperature is given in degrees Fahrenheit and Celsius. Baking pan measurements are in inches and centimetres as well as quarts and litres. An exact metric conversion is given below as well as the working equivalent (Standard Measure).

OVEN TEMPERATURES

Fahrenheit (°F)	Celsius (°C)
175°	80°
200°	95°
225°	110°
250°	120°
275°	140°
300°	150°
325°	160°
350°	175°
375°	190°
400°	205°
425°	220°
450°	230°
475°	240°
500°	260°

SPOONS

Conventional Measure	Metric Exact Conversion Millilitre (mL)	Metric Standard Measure Millilitre (mL)
1/8 teaspoon (tsp.)	0.6 mL	0.5 mL
1/4 teaspoon (tsp.)	1.2 mL	1 mL
1/2 teaspoon (tsp.)	2.4 mL	2 mL
1 teaspoon (tsp.)	4.7 mL	5 mL
2 teaspoons (tsp.)	9.4 mL	10 mL
1 tablespoon (tbsp.)	14.2 mL	15 mL

CUPS

Conventional Measure	Metric Exact Conversion Millilitre (mL)	Metric Standard Measure Millilitre (mL)
1/4 cup (4 tbsp.)	56.8 mL	60 mL
1/3 cup (5 1/3 tbsp.)	75.6 mL	75 mL
1/2 cup (8 tbsp.)	113.7 mL	125 mL
2/3 cup (10 2/3 tbsp.)	151.2 mL	150 mL
3/4 cup (12 tbsp.)	170.5 mL	175 mL
1 cup (16 tbsp.)	227.3 mL	250 mL
4 1/2 cups	1022.9 mL	1000 mL (1 L)

PANS

Conventional Inches	Metric Centimetres
8x8 inch	20x20 cm
9x9 inch	22x22 cm
9x13 inch	22x33 cm
10x15 inch	25x38 cm
11x17 inch	28x43 cm
8x2 inch round	20x5 cm
9x2 inch round	22x5 cm
10x4 1/2 inch tube	25x11 cm
8x4x3 inch loaf	20x10x7 cm
9x5x3 inch loaf	22x12x7 cm

DRY MEASUREMENTS

Conventional Measure Ounces (oz.)	Metric Exact Conversion Grams (g)	Metric Standard Measure Grams (g)
1 oz.	28.3 g	30 g
2 oz.	56.7 g	55 g
3 oz.	85.0 g	85 g
4 oz.	113.4 g	125 g
5 oz.	141.7 g	140 g
6 oz.	170.1 g	170 g
7 oz.	198.4 g	200 g
8 oz.	226.8 g	250 g
16 oz.	453.6 g	500 g
32 oz.	907.2 g	1000 g (1 kg)

CASSEROLES (Canada & Britain)

Standard Size Casserole	Exact Metric Measure
1 qt. (5 cups)	1.13 L
1 1/2 qts. (7 1/2 cups)	1.69 L
2 qts. (10 cups)	2.25 L
2 1/2 qts. (12 1/2 cups)	2.81 L
3 qts. (15 cups)	3.38 L
4 qts. (20 cups)	4.5 L
5 qts. (25 cups)	5.63 L

CASSEROLES (United States)

Standard Size Casserole	Exact Metric Measure
1 qt. (4 cups)	900 mL
1 1/2 qts. (6 cups)	1.35 L
2 qts. (8 cups)	1.8 L
2 1/2 qts. (10 cups)	2.25 L
3 qts. (12 cups)	2.7 L
4 qts. (16 cups)	3.6 L
5 qts. (20 cups)	4.5 L

Index

MAIL ORDER FORM

Buy 2 Get 1 FREE!
Buy 2 cookbooks—get 1 of equal value ABSOLUTELY FREE!

Tell us which book(s) you want FREE!
Mark "F" beside the title(s) of your choice.

Company's Coming cookbooks are available at retail locations everywhere!

$19.99 ASSORTED TITLES
*Also available in French

QUANTITY

	Company's Coming for Christmas* (hardcover)
NEW	Easy Entertaining* (hardcover, Oct 98)
	Beef Today! (softcover)

No. of Books Purchased [ ] X $19.99 = $ [ ]   No. of FREE Books [ ]

Choose 1 FREE book for every 2 books of equal value purchased

$14.99 ASSORTED TITLES
*Also available in French

QUANTITY

		QUANTITY	
	The Family Table		Kids Only - Snacks*
	Low-fat Cooking*	NEW	Company's Coming for Kids - Lunches (July 98)

No. of Books Purchased [ ] X $14.99 = $ [ ]   No. of FREE Books [ ]

Choose 1 FREE book for every 2 books of equal value purchased

$12.99 COMPANY'S COMING SERIES
*Also available in French

QUANTITY

		QUANTITY		QUANTITY		QUANTITY	
	150 Delicious Squares*		Vegetables		Microwave Cooking*		Breads*
	Casseroles*		Main Courses		Preserves*		Meatless Cooking*
	Muffins & More*		Pasta*		Light Casseroles*		Cooking For Two*
	Salads*		Cakes		Chicken, Etc.*		Breakfasts & Brunches*
	Appetizers		Barbecues*		Kids Cooking*	NEW	Slow Cooker Recipes (Sept 98)
	Desserts		Dinners of the World		Fish & Seafood*		
	Soups & Sandwiches		Lunches*				
	Holiday Entertaining*		Pies*				
	Cookies*		Light Recipes*				

No. of Books Purchased [ ] X $12.99 = $ [ ]   No. of FREE Books [ ]

Choose 1 FREE book for every 2 books of equal value purchased

$9.99 SELECT SERIES
*Also available in French

QUANTITY

		QUANTITY	
	Sauces & Marinades*		30-Minute Meals*
	Ground Beef*		Make-Ahead Salads*
	Beans & Rice*		No-Bake Desserts*

No. of Books Purchased [ ] X $9.99 = $ [ ]   No. of FREE Books [ ]

Choose 1 FREE book for every 2 books of equal value purchased

$4.99 PINT SIZE SERIES

QUANTITY

		QUANTITY	
	Finger Food		Baking Delights
	Buffets		Chocolate
	Party Planning		Beverages

No. of Books Purchased [ ] X $4.99 = $ [ ]   No. of FREE Books [ ]

Choose 1 FREE book for every 2 books of equal value purchased

---

Make cheque or money order payable to: **COMPANY'S COMING PUBLISHING LIMITED**
- **ORDERS OUTSIDE OF CANADA:** Must be paid in U.S. funds by cheque or money order drawn on Canadian or U.S. bank, or by credit card.
- Rush courier rates available on request. Please call our Shipping Department (403) 450-6223 for details.
- Prices subject to change without prior notice.
- Sorry, no C.O.D.'s.
- Bill my MasterCard or Visa (please check one) ○ MasterCard ○ VISA

_____ Expiry Date

Account # _____

Name of Cardholder _____

Cardholder's Signature _____

TOTAL PRICE FOR ALL BOOKS	$
Plus Shipping & Handling (for each destination)	$ 5.00
SUB-TOTAL	$
Canadian residents add G.S.T. / H.S.T. (7%)	$
TOTAL AMOUNT ENCLOSED	$

One low rate for shipping & handling—ANY SIZE ORDER!!

○ **YES! Please send a catalogue.** ○ **English** ○ **French**

Company's Coming cookbooks are available at retail locations everywhere. For information contact:

COMPANY'S COMING PUBLISHING LIMITED

Box 8037, Station "F"   Box 17870
Edmonton, Alberta   San Diego, California
Canada T6H 4N9   U.S.A. 92177-7870

TEL: (403) 450-6223
FAX: (403) 450-1857